Contents

1

Introduction:
Go **W***here* **with Baby?!**

Nobody told me that life as a new parent was going to be easy, but I was definitely not prepared for how challenging it was to simply **get out of the house with a baby** and do something fun together. What had been a quick stop at the grocery store after work suddenly became a major expedition once my son arrived. Besides getting him dressed and ready to go, I had to pack the **diaper bag**, prepare an **emergency bottle**, load the **stroller** into the car, and remember to bring the **shopping list,** which had grown far too long to keep in my head!

In time we did manage to master the grocery store routine though, and I started seeking out other activities to do with my new partner. Especially since I had recently left a hectic career for motherhood, the prospect of puttering around the house all day without any **adult conversation** was downright depressing.

So began my quest for interesting **baby friendly places**. But where could we go together that would tolerate **baby's occasional temper tantrums** or big, smelly poops? What places would be fun for both me *and* baby to visit? Where could we meet other new mommy and baby teams like ourselves to socialize with?

Fortunately **Long Island** boasts an abundance of **entertainment options** for little ones and their parents alike. On warm, sunny days, you can choose from a variety of **fair weather outings,** ranging from the magnificent grounds of former Gold Coast estates to cute petting zoos. **Chapter Three** reviews some of the **best outdoor spots** to explore. All have been "mom tested" and include **nearby dining options** when feasible.

Come winter, you don't have to feel stuck at home though. **Chapter Four** lists a number of **indoor escapes** to visit on a whim. Activities run the gamut, from **play spaces** and **puppet shows,** catering more to toddler tastes, to family-oriented museums of dual **interest to parents** and children.

If it's the pleasure of adult companionship that's desired, look up one of the social groups listed in **Chapter Five.** These terrific **"baby blues" busters** provide a relaxed and comfortable setting for bringing new parents together. The little ones can also benefit from social interactions with their "peers" and begin to learn interpersonal skills such as **sharing** and "playing nice in the sandbox."

When it's baby's turn for a little "intellectual stimulation," you'll find a diverse array of **classes** to kick start her **early education** in **Chapter Six**. Many of these **"mommy and me" classes** are offered to the **tiniest of infants** and provide a fun way for baby to "learn" while interacting with other children. In fact, mom or dad might pick up a few new tunes to continue the entertainment at home. I must admit, that as a **first-time mother**, I had no clue how to do the "Eentsy Weentsy Spider" until I learned it at one of these classes. I have since added countless other **songs and finger plays** to our daily repertoire that we still enjoy together.

Is it Baby Friendly?

In addition to listing the **address, phone, website,** and **fees,** the reviews include the following information to help parents gauge whether a particular place is baby friendly.

Baby Friendly Factors

Activities: Type of activities offered such as **classes, stroller walks, exhibits**, and toddler play areas.

Age: Recommended **minimum age** of child to participate in activity.

Timing: Hours and seasons of operation, times when **less crowded, special events** to watch for.

Duration: Approximate time it takes to enjoy the place without wearing out baby or yourself.

Finding It: Address and general **directions**, like **LIE exit** number and major access roads. Call or check their website for detailed directions.

Parking: Availability and **convenience** of parking.

Strollers: Ease of getting stroller into, and around the place, necessity of using steps.

Bathrooms: Presence of bathrooms & **diaper-changing** facilities.

Food: Availability of food for purchase and/or dining facilities where home-brought food can be consumed; nearby dining recommendations.

The *Big* Disclaimer

This book is by no means an exhaustive account of all the **parks, classes, museums**, and places that welcome babies. Rather my intention is to **create awareness** of the myriad possibilities out there for babies and their caregivers.

In addition, though this book is organized by type of activity – be it classes, play spaces, or mother discussion groups, many of the places reviewed offer multiple activities under one roof. To avoid being redundant, **each place is reviewed in depth only once** under the activity it's best known for.

Here Today, Gone Tomorrow

Finally, keep in mind that places come and go, and specifics like program features, operating hours, and **prices change frequently** so it's best to **call or log on for the latest information before visiting.**

Comments or suggestions for future editions? Let us know!

SCOPE
Education Services

SCOPE Publications
100 Lawrence Avenue
Smithtown, NY 11787
631-881-9650
www.scopeonline.us

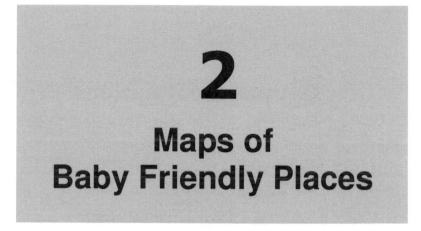

2

Maps of
Baby Friendly Places

Sounds great, but where is it?

Comprised of some **250 villages** stretching over 100 miles, L - o - n - g Island certainly lives up to its name. So when you hear of a potentially fun spot and are trying to decide whether to check it out with the kids, it's helpful to have a sense of where it is on the Island.

Fortunately most of the Island's villages can be grouped into one of **twelve "towns" (shown in the map below)**. Along with the exact address, the town is listed in the reviews to make it easier to figure out whether you'll be driving for half an hour or half a day. You can also thumb through all the **listings by town** in **Chapter Eight**.

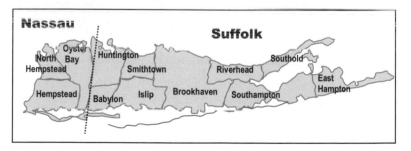

Outdoor Destinations

Nassau

1. Queens Zoo, p.22
2. Long Beach, p.46
3. Freeport Nautical Mile, p.60
4. Jones Beach, p.43
5. Great Neck Plaza, p.62
6. Old Westbury Gardens, p.34
7. Old Bethpage Restoration, p.64
8. Planting Fields Arboretum, p.36

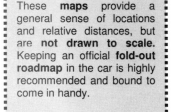

These **maps** provide a general sense of locations and relative distances, but are **not drawn to scale.** Keeping an official **fold-out roadmap** in the car is highly recommended and bound to come in handy.

Suffolk

9. Caumsett State Park, p.30
10. Cold Spring Harbor Hatchery, p.18
11. White Post Farms, p.24
12. Vanderbilt Mansion, p.40
13. Northport Village, p.57
14. Sunken Meadow State Park, p.54
15. Robert Moses State Park, p.52
16. Bayard Cutting Arboretum, p.28
17. Sailors Haven, Fire Island, p.49
18. Port Jefferson Village, p.70
19. Brookhaven Animal Preserve, p.26
20. Live Steamers, p.32
21. Animal Farm Petting Zoo, p.14
22. Long Island Game Farm, p.20
23. Atlantis Marine World, p.16
24. Quogue Wildlife Refuge, p.38
25. Sag Harbor Village, p.66

Indoor Escapes

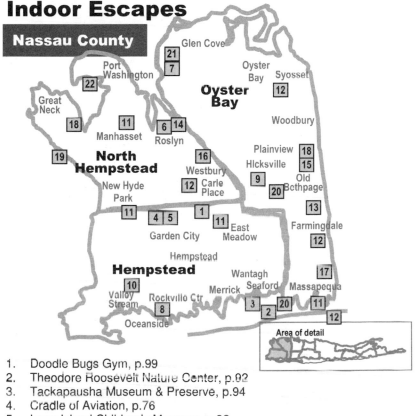

1. Doodle Bugs Gym, p.99
2. Theodore Roosevelt Nature Center, p.92
3. Tackapausha Museum & Preserve, p.94
4. Cradle of Aviation, p.76
5. Long Island Children's Museum, p.82
6. Nassau County Museum of Art, p.86
7. Garvies Point Museum, p.78
8. Center for Science & Learning, p.95
9. Long Island Puppet Theater, p.114
10. The Children's Safari, p.97
11. Barnes & Noble, p.122
12. Borders Books, p.122
13. Wood Kingdom, p.102
14. Active Kidz, p.98
15. Once Upon a Treetop, p.100
16. Orly's Treehouse, p.103
17. Bouncers & Slydos, p.109
18. Pump It Up, p.110
19. Alley Pond, p.158
20. Stroller Strides, p.159
21. Center for Parents, p.129
22. Parent Resource Ctr, p.130

Indoor Escapes

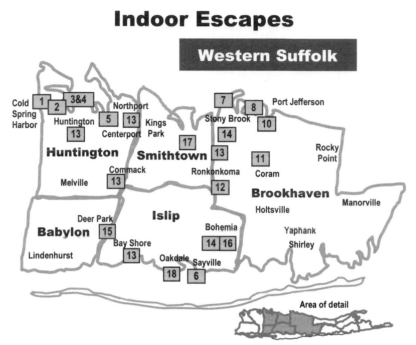

Western Suffolk

1. Cold Spring Harbor Fish Hatchery, p.18
2. Cold Spring Harbor Whaling Museum, p.75
3. Heckscher Museum of Art, p.80
4. Book Revue, p.122
5. Vanderbilt Mansion & Museum, p.40
6. Little Sunshine Playcenter, p.101
7. Long Island Museum of Art, History & Carriages, p.84
8. Children's Maritime Museum, p.91
9. Let's Bounce 'N' Party, p.106
10. Fun 4 All, p.111
11. Wood Kingdom, p.102
12. Jump, p.107
13. Barnes & Noble, p.122
14. Borders Books, p.122
15. Kangaroo Kids, p.108
16. Pump It Up, p.110
17. Caleb Smith State Park, p.154
18. Connetquot River State Park, p.155

Indoor Escapes

Out East

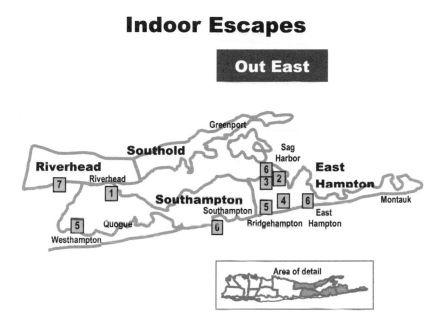

1. Atlantis Marine World, p.16
2. Goat On A Boat Puppet Theater, p.112
3. Sag Harbor Whaling Museum, p.88
4. Children's Museum of the East End, p.90
5. The Open Book, p.122
6. BookHampton, p.122
7. Borders Books, p.122

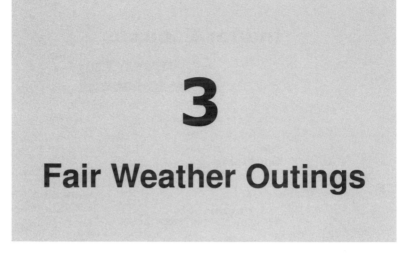

3

Fair Weather Outings

It's warm, the sun is shining, and you have the whole day ahead of you – time to take the little one outside! This chapter offers a sampler of terrific, baby friendly outdoor destinations including petting zoos, arboretums, nature preserves, beaches, and quaint tourist towns.

Savings for Frequent Drivers

If you anticipate being out a lot, it's definitely worth investing in an **Empire Passport.** For $65, the parking sticker entitles you to a year of **unlimited access** to New York State parks. There are **about 20** on Long Island, half of which are reviewed in this book. Many of these parks have wonderful, **inexpensive nature programs** for children too.

To obtain a sticker and see a listing of all the NY State Parks on Long Island, go to **www.nysparks.com**. The Empire Passport is also for sale at the ticket booths of most state parks so you can pick one up on your next visit.

Animal Kingdoms

Isn't it amazing how early babies begin to respond to animals? From **peacocks to pigs, tigers to turtles,** almost any moving creature seems to capture their interest, and you can find **hundreds of exotic species** right here on the island. Sure, there's that fabulous zoo in the Bronx, but if you don't feel like dealing with the **bridges, tolls, and traffic,** give some of the places listed in this section a try. Baby can even get **up close and personal** with some of the more mild-mannered creatures at the **petting zoos** which offer plenty of opportunities to **feed** friendly farm animals.

Reviewed in This Section

- Animal Farm Petting Zoo
- Atlantis Marine World
- Brookhaven Animal Preserve
- Cold Spring Harbor Fish Hatchery
- Long Island Game Farm
- Queens Zoo
- White Post Farms

Visit Tip: bring wipes for baby's hands after touching the animals – those furry creatures are cute, but they don't bathe nearly as often as we do!

Animal Farm Petting Zoo

296 Wading River Road, Manorville
Suffolk, Town of Brookhaven
631-878-1785
www.afpz.org

Activities: Petting zoo, toddler play area, live shows, pony rides & children's train ride.

Age: About 10 months and up.

Timing: Open Spring through Fall, Mon-Fri, 10-5pm, Sat & Sun, 10-6pm; call for exact dates of operation.

Duration: 1-4 hours.

Fees: Adults, $13.50; ages 2+, $11.50; under 2, free. Rides, shows and other attractions included in admission price.

Finding It: LIE to exit 69, head south on Wading River Rd for ~2.5 miles, entrance will be on the right.

Parking: Very good, large lot right by the entrance.

Strollers: Entire grounds completely stroller-accessible.

Bathrooms: Restrooms have diaper changing tables.

Food: Order from the snack bar or bring your own and eat at their picnic tables.

The Scoop:

Don't forget the camera! At this cute petting zoo, your toddler can experience the sensation of **goats nibbling food pellets right out of her hand**, and you'll definitely want to capture her delighted expression on film!

In addition to the myriad gentle *farm* animals that welcome baby's touch, the zoo also houses a motley crew of the more rancorous members of the animal kingdom including **monkeys, camels, and parrots** - all living in fairly natural, spacious habitats.

Visit Tip:

Bring **reading material** - the play area towards the back can keep tiny tots occupied in a pretty safe environment, allowing you to sit back, relax, and maybe flip through a magazine while they frolic within eyesight.

In fact, we were pleasantly surprised by how extensive the facilities were, especially after driving up to the deceptively-modest storefront claiming to be a petting zoo. But we quickly discovered a wide variety of activities to keep toddler entertained such as **kiddy rides**, **shows**, and a **playground** – all included in the admission price. We also made excellent time getting there on the LIE, making the trip worthwhile, and I would even recommend it to families living in Nassau County.

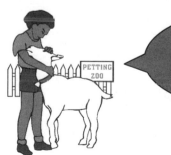

Let's make a playdate! Meet inside the gift shop where you buy the tickets.

Atlantis Marine World

431 East Main Street, Riverhead
Suffolk, Town of Riverhead
631-208-9200
www.atlantismarineworld.com

Activities: Aquarium with large collection of sea creatures, animal feedings and shows.

Age: About 8 months on up; colorful exhibits are fascinating for toddlers, but watch your back! Several tanks are too high up for toddler to see unless lifted by an adult.

Timing: Open year-round, daily, 10-5pm; indoor exhibits make it a good rainy day destination but more to see outdoors in nice weather.

Duration: 1-3 hours.

Fees: Adults, $21; children 3-17, $18; under 3, free.

Finding It: LIE to exit 71; Take Rte 94/24 east about 3.5 miles and follow signs to parking lot.

Parking: Decent, although parking lot can be about a 5 minute walk to the entrance depending on how close your spot is.

Stroller: Completely stroller-accessible; elevator available to reach second floor.

Food: Cafeteria with basic lunch food or bring your own to eat in the large dining area.

Bathrooms: Diaper changing table in the ladies room.

The Scoop:

Ben was just nine months old when I first took him to this **aquarium** located where the two "forks" of Long Island meet. At that tender age, he was in no position to tell apart a **horseshoe crab** from a **sea horse**, but he did respond to the large **sharks gliding by** in their tank just a couple feet from his face. When we visited again about a year later however, he was completely entranced by the **diverse and colorful marine life**. I appreciated that he was able to see some of the exhibits from the comfort of his stroller although a number of the tanks were so high, **he had to be lifted up to get a peek.**

While the large space has enough to keep you busy **indoors** on a crummy day, there are even more things to see in good weather. The **outdoor sea lion show** for example, is fun and included in the admission price. It may be worth consulting the aquarium's website for **show times** so you can time your trip accordingly.

Attention Shoppers!

About a five minute drive from the aquarium is the **Tanger Outlet Center**. This huge **outdoor mall** has over **150 stores** and is **open daily** until at least **8pm**. Beware, it's quite popular, and can get pretty **crowded**.

Tanger Outlet Center
1770 West Main St, Riverhead
LIE Exit 73, 800-407-4894

Anyone even remotely interested in fish will enjoy a visit to **Atlantis Marine World**. And though it's almost the last exit off the LIE, **the road trip goes by surprisingly fast** so don't let the seemingly far distance deter you from visiting.

Let's make a playdate! Meet by the stingray tank just past ticket booth (before the bridge).

Cold Spring Harbor Fish Hatchery

1660 Rte 25A, Cold Spring Harbor
Suffolk, Town of Huntington
516-692-6768
www.cshfha.org

Activities: Fish hatchery; other live animals on display.

Age: Good for young children since many of the reptiles, amphibians and fish are housed in tanks low to the ground at toddler eye-level; step stools provided to gain access to higher tanks, and climbing up them is half the fun!
Less interesting for small babies.

Timing: Open daily 10-5pm, year-round.

Duration: About an hour.

Fees: Adults, $5; children 3-17, $3; under 3, free.

Finding It: LIE to exit 41N (Rte 106/Oyster Bay), follow Rte 106 north about 3.5 miles, turn left at light onto Rte 25A/Northern Blvd. Go approx. 3.7 miles to entrance on right side.

Parking: Very good; parking lot right by the entrance.

Stroller: Very good; completely stroller-accessible.

Bathrooms: Bathrooms across the street in smaller building, no diaper changing facilities.

Food: None served; okay to bring food to eat at picnic tables out back, or head over to Cold Spring Harbor Village, about 1 mile east on 25A (Main St); several cafés there serve sandwiches, coffee & snacks. Take your pick, they are all good.

The Scoop:

Straddling the border of Nassau and Suffolk counties, this century old **fish hatchery** still churns out thousands of trout every year for release in nearby ponds. **Outdoors** you will find a number **of "trout-rearing" pools**, where you and baby can trace the stages of a trout's development from a tiny minnow to a full-fledged adult. And don't forget to inquire about "Tiny" the absolutely **humongous snapping turtle** that resides in the stream out back!

Let's make a playdate! Meet inside the building where you buy the tickets.

Indoors, you will discover a diverse array of slimy, scaly, slithering creatures, including **frogs, turtles and fish**. The two buildings containing these live exhibits are pretty compact as well, so it's easy to keep track of wandering toddlers.

Making a Day Out of It

Since it doesn't take very long to tour the premises, you might consider walking up to the picturesque 19th century **church** about 100 yards behind the hatchery. It overlooks a pretty **pond** that seems to be a popular hangout for swans as well as their young human spectators in strollers.

Day-trippers might even consider driving into the **historic village of Cold Spring Harbor** which is lined with quaint shops and is home to the **Whaling Museum** that's also reviewed in this book.

Long Island Game Farm Wildlife Park

Chapman Boulevard, Manorville
Suffolk, Town of Brookhaven
631-878-6644
www.longislandgamefarm.com

Activities: Zoo in park-like setting with wide variety of animals, kiddie rides, live animal shows.

Age: About 10 months & up to enjoy animals. Terrific for toddlers; many opportunities to pet and feed animals; wonderful carousel and kiddie train ride – but it's easy to lose sight of a wandering child on the large, open grounds.

Timing: Open daily Memorial Day through Labor Day, From 10am to 5 or 6pm depending on the season. Call or check website for exact dates or operation and animal show times before going.

Duration: 2-4 hours.

Fees: Varies by season - Adults, ~$16-$18; children 3-11, $14-$16; under 3, free. All rides, shows, and attractions included in admission price.

Finding It: Exit 70 off LIE; Take Rte 111 south, after ½ mile make right onto Chapman Blvd; entrance is approx. 2 miles down on the left.

Parking: Very good; large dedicated parking lot right by entrance.

Stroller: Excellent; completely stroller-accessible.

Bathrooms: Diaper changing table in the restroom.

Food: Snack bar serving hot dogs etc., or bring your own food to eat at their shaded picnic tables.

The Scoop:

Although **Manorville** may seem like a long haul for folks living in Nassau, keep in mind it's a **straight shot on the LIE** and probably takes less time to get to than the traffic-congested area surrounding the Bronx Zoo, with a lot less hassles. And while the scope and scale of this zoo doesn't compare to its counterpart in the Bronx, there are plenty of opportunities for baby to meet **exotic animals in fairly close quarters.**

Bambiland, for example, was a big hit with my toddler who frolicked among a herd of friendly deer without any barriers like cages or fences. He was less inclined however, to **pet the baby alligator** carried around by a staff member for visitors to touch. That was just fine by me though, because I wasn't feeling particularly inspired to stroke a scaly reptile either.

The live **tiger show** however, was very exciting and there were many **awe-struck toddlers** present the day we visited. In fact I counted about a dozen strollers parked outside the **open-air amphitheater** where they performed.

While it's a far cry from the jungle, the grounds are tastefully designed, with an eye toward maintaining a **natural habitat** for their wild residents. Connected by a series of tree-lined boardwalks and nature trails, the animal exhibits are fairly spread out as well, making it a pleasant place to take a leisurely stroll. And while you're there, don't forget to visit the **monkeys**; babies and toddlers seem to love watching their silly antics!

Queens Zoo

53-51 111th Street (at 53rd Avenue)
Flushing Meadows Corona Park, Queens
718-271-1500
www.queenszoo.com

Activities: Wildlife park, petting zoo, carousel, nearby playground.

Age: Stroller-bound babies and up. Zoo space is enclosed enough to keep track of roaming toddlers. A few of the animals can be hard to spot sometimes in their natural habitats. The domed aviary has an ascending paved ramp that is fun to run up.

Timing: Open year-round, daily, 10-4:30 or 5:30pm; zoo and surrounding park are teeming with school children at certain times of the year so go after 2pm weekdays to avoid competing with them for a view of the animals.

Duration: 1 – 2 hours.

Fees: Adults, $7; children 3-12, $3; under 3, free.

Finding It: LIE to Exit 22A (108th St) *Green signs for the zoo will help guide you.* Make right onto 108th St; go about 8 blocks and make right onto 52nd Ave; go 1 block and make right onto 111th St. Parking lot is on left. Park at the **end of lot at 56th St** to be close to ramp entrance.

Parking: Parking lot is fairly large and getting a spot is generally not a problem on weekdays.

Stroller: Completely stroller-accessible.

Bathrooms: Bathrooms at the petting zoo and toward the back of wildlife preserve. Both have diaper changing facilities in ladies room.

Food: No food served on zoo grounds - just a few vending machines in the outdoor dining area (across from the seals in wildlife preserve). OK to bring your own food to eat at their shaded tables. Or stop by the carousel just before zoo entrance where there's usually a hotdog and/or ice cream vendor.

The Scoop:

O.K., technically it's *not* in Nassau County, but the zoo's convenient location near exits off the **LIE** and **Northern State Parkway** makes it a surprisingly short drive, traffic permitting of course. And although I have gotten stuck on the expressway trying to get there, *and* it does take awhile to walk from the parking lot to the ticket booth, I still think animal-loving toddlers deserve a trip to the **Queens Zoo**.

But don't expect to find giraffes, zebras, or other exotic species from far-flung continents like Africa. This is strictly the domain of North **American** wildlife. Here your child will discover "new world" animals such as **coyotes, panthers,** and the **California sea lions** who are fun to watch at feeding time.

Let's make a playdate! Meet in shaded dining area across from the sea lions.

Across from the wildlife preserve is the **petting zoo**, and your ticket gets you into both places. Be sure to remember which pocket you stuck it in; I had to rummage around to find mine!

White Post Farms

250 Old Country Road, Melville
Suffolk, Town of Huntington
631-351-9373, 72
www.whitepostfarms.com

Activities: Petting zoo, playground, pony rides.

Age: About 9 months and up. Toddlers and older children will enjoy the ride and playground.

Timing: Open late Spring to late Fall, daily, 11-5pm.

Duration: 1-3 hours.

Fees: Adults & children for outdoor, $7; under 2, free. Pony ride and train rides are additional. Printable discount coupons on website.

Finding It: LIE to exit 49N, take Rte 110 north. At first light, turn right onto Old Country Rd. Farm is 1/4 mile down on the right.

Parking: Very good, large, dedicated parking lot near the entrance, spillover parking field around corner.

Stroller: Very good, no steps, wide paths are stroller-accessible, grass and gravel in some places makes the pushing a little harder.

Bathrooms: Diaper changing table in the bathroom.

Food: Snack bar serves lunch basics, or bring your own food and eat at one of the many picnic tables on the grounds.

The Scoop:

On a nice day, **White Post Farms** is a pleasant spot to take baby or toddler to meet furry, four-legged friends. Although it's **attractive landscaping**, grassy lawns, and manicured flower beds don't exactly conjure up images of a typical farm, the **plgs, chickens, cows** and other domesticated animals compensate quite nicely.

Here you can see barely-toddling youngsters giggle with delight as goats lick food pellets off their stubby little fingers. Thrill-seeking older toddlers go for the **train rides;** tickets can be purchased at the main entrance for $2. There are a number of **coin-operated kiddie rides** as well, so stock up on quarters if that's your thing.

The highlight of the visit for my 20 month old son however, was the playground where he spent a solid hour climbing all over **big, wooden pirate ships, buses, tractors**, and other forms of transportation. I had my 4 month old infant with me, and took the time to snuggle with him on the spacious lawn while watching his older brother play.

In a somewhat contained, park-like setting, White Post Farms is also an ideal outing for **grandparents**.

Brookhaven Animal Preserve

249 Buckley Road, Holtsville
Suffolk, Town of Brookhaven
631-758-9664 for Preserve
www.brookhaven.org, click on Wildlife & Ecology Center
or do a web search of Brookhaven Animal Preserve

Activities: Zoo, petting zoo, and playground.

Age: About 7 months and up.

Timing: Open year-round, daily, 9-4pm.

Duration: An hour or a whole afternoon.

Fees: Free!

Finding It: LIE to exit 63; head south on County Rd 83/North Ocean Ave. At 4th light (~2 miles), turn right onto Rte 99/Woodside Ave. At 2nd road, turn right onto Buckley Rd. Parking lot on right.

Parking: Very good; large lot right by entrance.

Stroller: Excellent; completely stroller accessible.

Bathrooms: Diaper changing tables in men's *and* ladies room in the greenhouse. Dads take note!

Food: Bring food to eat at outdoor picnic area; snack bar serves burgers in warm weather.

The Scoop:

This zoo is a fun, economical place to introduce baby to the world of animals. **Mountain lions, black bear** and **bobcats** roam here in habitats that enable fairly close encounters with the wildlife.

Right beside the animal preserve is a large **playground** that features an impressive collection of swings, slides and climbing equipment. It's conveniently located near the **concession stand** so parents can observe little ones from the comfort of a **picnic table**.

Lovely Landscapes

Long Island has had its share of ultra-wealthy business tycoons over the past couple centuries, and many have left behind legacies in the form of **enormous estates**. Featuring magnificent mansions, gorgeous **formal gardens**, and **lush greenhouses**, these properties have been painstakingly maintained over the years, and still radiate much of their original splendor.

Now turned over to various government bodies and historic trusts, these former stomping grounds of **the rich and famous** are open to the public and welcome parents to bring their kids along **for a stroller ride**. This section covers some of the more baby friendly estates, as well as a couple of other lovely landscapes that were never the domain of the moneyed few, but worth visiting for their unique appeal.

Reviewed In This Section

- Bayard Cutting Arboretum
- Caumsett State Historic Park
- Live Steamers at Southaven County Park
- Old Westbury Gardens
- Planting Fields Arboretum
- Quogue Wildlife Refuge & Nature Center
- Vanderbilt Mansion & Museum

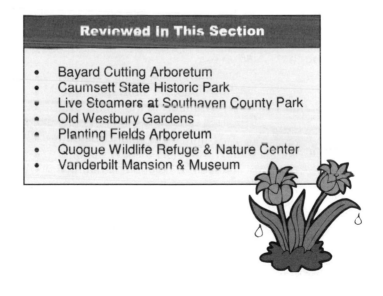

Bayard Cutting Arboretum

Montauk Highway, Oakdale
Suffolk, Town of Islip
631-581-1002
www.bayardcuttingarboretum.com

Activities: Beautiful grounds to explore with baby.

Age: Babies on up; lots of space outdoors for toddler to roam, though mansion not really of interest to toddler so bring toys to keep him or her occupied in the café.

Timing: Grounds & mansion open Tue-Sun, 10-5pm, year-round; nice to visit when Café open as well, hours 11am to about 4pm.

Duration: 1-4 hours.

Fees: Vehicle fee: $6 in summer; no charge with Empire Passport sticker and off-season.

Finding It: LIE to exit 53S, take Sagtikos Pkwy south (follow signs for Southern State Pkwy east, & Heckscher State Pkwy); take exit 45E for Montauk Hwy (Rte 27A). Follow signs to Arboretum. Entrance approx. 0.4 miles down on right.

Parking: Good, large lot right by mansion entrance is pretty empty weekdays but can fill up on nice weekends.

Stroller: Great; mansion & café are stroller-accessible, most paths paved, waterside path is pebbly but navigable with a stroller & worth extra pushing.

Bathrooms: No diaper changing facilities, ladies room in mansion is spacious enough to improvise.

Food: No picnicking allowed on grounds but mansion café serves reasonably-priced coffee, and lunch items.

The Scoop:

Set on the shores of the **Connetquot River**, the **Bayard Cutting Arboretum** features extensive, well-manicured grounds to explore with little ones. Baby and I strolled easily along the mostly flat, paved paths and passed a surprising variety of habitats ranging from **wetland marshes** to **evergreen woods** to a **quiet waterfront**.

While the lovely gardens of the Arboretum especially beckon in late spring when the flowers bloom, a visit with bundled-up baby **off-season** can also yield botanical surprises such as brilliant autumn leaves. And when it gets too chilly out, you can duck into the **café,** which serves coffee and light lunches year-round. (It's also spacious enough to accommodate strollers.) Overlooking a grand lawn, the café also **has outdoor seating** along the mansion's wrap-around porch.

Let's make a playdate! Meet in the café inside the mansion.

But if you simply want to relax outdoors in a serene setting, make a bee-line to the river; there are plenty of park **benches along the water's edge** where you and baby can mellow out for a while.

29

Caumsett State Historic Park

25 Lloyd Harbor Road, Huntington
Suffolk, Town of Huntington
631-423-1770
www.nysparks.state.ny.us/parks
Select Caumsett from drop down menu

Activities: Bike riding & strolling on flat, paved paths, small bird sanctuary, horse stables.

Age: Stroller-bound infants on up; lots of open space for toddler to run around, but watch out for the goose poop!

Timing: Open daily, sunrise to sunset, year-round.

Duration: 1 hour or a whole afternoon.

Fees: Vehicle fee $6, May-Columbus Day; no charge with Empire Passport sticker.

Finding It: LIE exit 45N; take Woodbury Rd north about 7 miles to intersection with Main St (25A), cross and continue for another 4-5 miles, (name changes to West Neck Rd); pass LI Sound on left, and look for entrance to Caumsett on left.

Parking: Large lot can get pretty full on beautiful weekends but you can always find a spot.

Stroller: Perfect; wide, paved roads with very restricted access to cars.

Bathrooms: No changing tables in the restrooms, improvise in the parking lot.

Food: None served; outside food welcome but no picnic tables - bring a blanket if you want to sprawl out on the grass with baby.

The Scoop:

Avid shoppers may appreciate the contributions made by **Marshall Field** to the development of the modern department store, but nature enthusiasts will certainly sing his praises for creating the lovely bucolic landscape that comprises **Caumsett State Historic Park**.

Let's make a playdate! Meet under Visitor Information Kiosk by parking lot .

Virtually free of any vehicular traffic, the flat, paved roads that wind around the property provide an ideal setting for introducing toddler to a **safe bike ride**. Jogging strollers are a common sight here as well, especially on the **3.5 mile loop** which passes serene meadows, forest-shaded paths, and culminates in a **panoramic view of Long Island Sound**.

Little ones will enjoy watching the **well-groomed horses** milling around their stables. They can also check out the smattering of injured **birds of prey** housed in cages just across from the ticket booth at the main entrance.

You won't have to look too hard though, to spot the **Canada geese** that flock to the park's large grassy areas in season. There's no escaping the goose turd either; it's everywhere, so be prepared to scrape it off the soles of baby's shoes before getting in the car.

Quite a bit of property hugs the shoreline, and if you're willing to push the stroller over two miles of bumpy dirt paths, you'll be rewarded by a lovely, albeit **pebbly, beach** where you and baby can gaze across the water to Connecticut.

Live Steamers

175 Gerrard Road, Yaphank
Suffolk, Town of Brookhaven
631-345-0499
www.trainweb.org/lils

Activities: Miniature train rides, picnicking facilities.

Age: About 18 months on up; toddling train enthusiasts will love this place!

Timing: Open late May through October, on alternating Sundays, 10:30-3pm; call or log on for specifics.

Duration: 1-2 hours.

Fees: Free! Donations welcome.

Finding It: Directions on website; **from LIE** take exit 68S (to William Floyd Pkwy/Shirley); make first right onto William Floyd Pkwy South (Rte 46); after about 3 miles, turn right at light onto Rte 27/**Sunrise Hwy** west (also called Victory Ave); go about 1 mile (passing Southaven Park's main entrance) and turn right onto Gerrard Rd. Continue about ½ mile and turn right at Live Steamer and Equestrian Center entrance. Make immediate right turn into grassy parking lot. **From Sunrise Hwy** take exit 58N, head west on Victory Ave and follow directions above.

Parking: Decent, long grassy parking lot near entrance; it can get tight at times, but spots turn over fast.

Stroller: O.K., woodchip and dirt paths are not ideal but that doesn't seem to stop parents from strolling around.

Bathrooms: "Port-A-John" behind the snack bar, no diaper changing facilities.

Food: Snack bar serves basics like burgers & hotdogs. Lots of picnic tables on site to eat a bagged lunch, but some reserved for **kid's birthdays**.

The Scoop:

If they can walk, they can ride! Those are the rules for tiny tots looking to board one of the **model trains** operated by the **Live Steamers**, a club for railroad hobbyists interested in steam power.

On **"run days,"** club members welcome the public to climb aboard their fine collection of model choo choos, and take an open-air ride through the forest. Club members donning engineer caps serve as the **train conductors** and even little Tycho, my 15 month old son, seemed to appreciate being a passenger on this wonderful miniature railroad.

My three year old however, was nothing short of smitten with the trains. He simply couldn't get enough, and I was glad the **rides were free** (in exchange, the club doesn't owe rent to Suffolk County for keeping their railroad on their property). Not surprisingly, the Steamers **draw large crowds** on nice days but fortunately the line for the train ride moves fairly rapidly.

===

Toddler's Turn to "Let Off Steam"

The Victory Avenue entrance to Southaven Park has extensive picnicking facilities, modern bathrooms, a lake and a playground for little ones. It can get pretty swamped in summer but it's a good option for something else to do that's close by. ($5 Fee)

===

Old Westbury Gardens

71 Old Westbury Road, Old Westbury
Nassau, Town of North Hempstead
516-333-0048
www.oldwestburygardens.org

Activities: Formal gardens, outdoor café, large open lawns, mansion tours, but strollers must be left outside.

Age: Stroller babies on up; great wide open spaces for children to roam; mansion mainly of adult interest; toddler-size log cabins are inviting for little ones to explore.

Timing: Open 10-5pm every day **except Tues.** April-Oct. (check for exact dates of operation).

Duration: 2-3 hours on a nice day.

Fees: Adults, $10; children 7-12, $5; 6 & under, free.

Finding It: From West: LIE exit 39, left onto Glen Cove Rd; cross over highway & make quick left onto service road. Go east about a mile and turn right onto Old Westbury Rd. Enter .4 miles up on left.

From East: LIE Exit 39 (Glen Cove Rd). Follow service road east about 1 mile; turn right onto Old Westbury Rd; entrance is about ½ mile further on left.

Parking: Get there early for nearby parking. Parking lot is about a five minute walk to the gardens.

Stroller: Can be rigorous on the mainly gravel and grass paths but worth the effort. Strollers welcome at outdoor café but not permitted in mansion.

Bathrooms: No diaper changing facilities in restrooms, though it's being considered for the future. Plenty of lawn space to improvise.

Food: Outdoor Café with seating. Outside food welcome in café and at picnic table area.

The Scoop:

A regal mansion perched atop several rolling acres of gently sloping lawns, **Old Westbury Gardens** is so picturesque, it seems like the set for a movie. And in fact it did serve as the backdrop for films shot by two great Hollywood directors, **Martin Scorcese** and **Alfred Hitchcock.**

Toddlers however, will revel in the extensive network of pathways leading to **ponds and maze-like flower gardens.** There's even a special **children's play area** featuring **pee wee-sized miniature log cabins** that will likely tempt yours to peek inside.

Strollers (and toddling feet) are welcome anywhere on the grounds. And even though pushing a stroller can be challenging at times along the gravel paths, it's absolutely essential to bring one to cover the extensive property. There are occasional steps to contend with also, but usually they can be circumvented by going on the grass. Strollers are not permitted however, **inside the mansion,** which can be visited via **guided tour.** That was O.K. with us though, because the gardens alone are reason enough to make a visit.

Planting Fields
Arboretum State Park

1395 Planting Fields Road Oyster Bay
Nassau, Town of Oyster Bay
516-922-9200
www.plantingfields.com

Activities: Formal gardens, greenhouse, extensive stroller-friendly paths, picnicking on the great lawns, trees bearing name plates that provide a crash course in botany.

Age: Stroller-bound infants on up; they can sleep while you enjoy the view; terrific for small children; wide open spaces for toddler to roam.

Timing: Grounds open year-round, daily from 9-5pm, greenhouses open 10-4pm.

Duration: 1-4 hours.

Fees: $6 vehicle fee during summer, weekends, and holidays; free with Empire State Passport and off season.

Finding It: Exit 41N off LIE; follow Rte 106 north for a couple miles. At the big intersection with a traffic light, make left onto Northern Blvd (25A west). Make first right onto Mill River Rd; follow signs for Planting Fields.

Parking: Very good during off-peak times like weekdays; lot gets full on sunny weekends.

Stroller: Great – a couple miles of paved roads for strolling; main greenhouse completely stroller-accessible; a few areas such as the formal gardens have rough paths that can be mildly challenging with a stroller.

Bathrooms: Diaper changing tables in both ladies & men's room. Located across from main greenhouse.

Food: None served but picnicking permitted at outdoor tables and on large grassy lawns; For **nearby family-friendly restaurant** try **IHOP**, 6281 Northern Blvd, East Norwich (between Mill River Rd and Rte 106), 516-922-8080.

The Scoop:

Once the exclusive **Gold Coast estate** of the business tycoon William Coe, Planting Fields Arboretum now welcomes the public to tour its **gorgeous gardens** and marvelous **collection of trees from all over the world**. You can lay a blanket almost anywhere on the grass, enjoy a picnic lunch, and surround yourselves with nature's splendors.

While the floral displays are at their finest during Spring and Summer, I find myself bringing the children to Planting Fields In **wintertime** as well. It's then when we escape to the **greenhouse**, a lush, tropical oasis that serves as the perfect antidote to the winter doldrums. Benches ring the perimeter, and there's nothing like snuggling with baby amidst the huge palms and **exotic plants,** knowing that the ground outside is covered with snow.

Let's make a playdate! Meet inside the main greenhouse next to the gift shop.

Quogue Wildlife Refuge & Nature Center

3 Old Country Road, Quogue
Suffolk, Town of Southampton
631-653-4771
www.quoguewildliferefuge.com

Activities: Trails, small wildlife sanctuary, nature center.

Age: Infants in baby carriers & up. Easy, flat trail for aspiring young hikers.

Timing: Trails & wildlife refugo opcn daily dawn to dusk, year-round. Nature center generally open Sat, Sun, Tue & Thu, 11-4pm, call to confirm. Note: it's nice to time visit for when nature center is open as well to see exhibits and have access to bathrooms.

Duration: 1-2 hours.

Fees: Free.

Finding It: LIE to exit 70S, Take Rte 111 south; make left onto Sunrise Hwy (Rte 27); take exit 64S and go south on Rte 104. After approx. 2 miles turn right onto Old Country Rd. Go approx. 0.7 miles to entrance on the right side.

Parking: Good, parking lot right by the entrance; additional parking across the street.

Stroller: Dirt and woodchip trails can be a bit tough with strollers; baby carriers are more convenient.

Bathrooms: Restrooms in nature center, no diaper changing facilities though.

Food: None served, picnicking prohibited in the
nature preserve.

The Scoop:

Although the woodchip covered trails can be somewhat challenging to navigate with a stroller, the **Quogue Wildlife Refuge** can easily be explored on foot with baby in a **front or back carrier**. Toddlers will also enjoy meandering along the flat paths which loop around unspoiled **woodlands, ponds, and marshes.**

As you enter the preserve, you will see the **distressed wildlife complex,** where little ones can experience close encounters with an **eagle, fox,** or other local animals whose injuries preclude them from surviving in the wild. Stuck in a cage they are, but that didn't stop one **wild turkey** from proudly strutting his stuff and squawking at my amused toddler.

Once on the trails, you will encounter a large, **picturesque pond,** a favorite watering hole for visiting fowl. Surrounded by dense forest, the pond's banks offer an intimate setting to relax and discover the world of nature with a little one.

The trails are pretty much always open, but you might want to time your visit to coincide with the hours of the adjacent nature center. Overlooking the pond, the **nature center** houses a curious assortment of stuffed animals including a seal and bear. Who knows, maybe this odd display of **taxidermy** is a tribute to the local hunters who were actually partly responsible for creating the preserve to provide a safe haven for ducks and other overly hunted wildlife.

Though not ideal for strollers and lacking in diaper-changing facilities, the Quogue Wildlife Refuge is worth checking out **if you happen to be in the area.** Happy trails!

Vanderbilt Mansion & Museum

180 Little Neck Road, Centerport
Suffolk, Town of Huntington
631-854-5555
www.vanderbiltmuseum.org

Activities: Former Gold Coast estate of adult interest.

Age: Stroller-bound infants on up; interesting animal exhibits at toddler's eye level in parts of the mansion. But the entire mansion can only be seen via guided tour which involves lots of steps and is not terribly thrilling for young children.

Timing: Open year-round, Tue-Sun, 12-5pm; hours vary slightly by season, check before visiting. This is a fair weather outing due to significant outdoor walking, but the indoor exhibits offer a fun **rainy day escape for locals.**

Duration: 1-2 hours.

Fees: Adults, $7; children under 12, $3.

Finding It: Exit 51off LIE. Take Deer Park Ave north to Park Ave. At 3rd light, turn right onto Broadway, go about 4.5 miles (crossing over 25A) onto Little Neck Rd. Entrance is ~1.5 miles up on the right.

Parking: Decent – plenty of spots in the lot but it's about a 5 minute stroll to the sites.

Stroller: Ground floor of certain buildings is stroller-accessible, no strollers allowed on mansion tour.

Bathrooms: Ladies room in planetarium has large counter top for changing baby; no diaper changing facilities in the restrooms in the mansion.

Food: No food permitted in the buildings; bring your own to eat at the outdoor picnic tables or see review of **Northport Village** for dining options.

The Scoop:

Be prepared to walk because the buildings comprising the former estate of William K. Vanderbilt II are sprawled out over several acres. A stroller is a 'must' here as even the mobile, older toddler will likely tire out touring the moderately hilly grounds that include a **mansion, marine museum**, and **planetarium**.

The mansion features an impressive collection of well-preserved animal and aquatic specimens from all over the world. Set low to the ground for convenient toddler viewing, the colorful exotic birds on display are particularly fascinating to little ones, and babies can enjoy unobstructed, close-up views from their strollers.

If you're up for seeing some **big game**, ask for the **Stoll Wing**. It's an adventure in itself to descend the narrow stairs leading into this small, dimly-lit extension of the mansion. In this cave-like setting, you and toddler will encounter some of the more ferocious members of the wild kingdom, including **lions, tigers, and bears...Oh My!** Be forewarned; it could be a very exciting place or pretty creepy depending on your child's outlook.

The **planetarium**, where the admission tickets are purchased, holds frequent **sky shows** in its domed theater. Though several shows are geared toward younger audiences, my toddler took one look at the dark theater and ran away hollering. But your toddler's response may be more favorable; if not, there's still much to discover at the adjacent museums, be it **snakes, starfish, or sea gulls**.

Beaches with Boardwalks

No matter where you live on Long Island, you're never very far from a beach. The trick is finding a baby friendly beach, that is, one with convenient parking, decent restrooms, a snack bar, and maybe even a little playground for the kiddies.

It's also nice to be able to take baby for a stroller ride along the water which makes **beaches with boardwalks** particularly appealing. If you grew up on the island, you probably have a favorite town beach you frequent. But knowing a few different beaches within an hour radius can lend some variety to the steady heat of summer.

While a day at the beach naturally springs to mind during the dog days of summer, I have found that **off-season** trips can be equally rewarding, and so much less crowded! And since most beaches don't require a **town permit** for access **after Labor Day**, you can go almost anywhere and find **parking right by the sand**. Then when you need to change baby's diaper, the car is just steps away.

Reviewed in This Section
• Jones Beach State Park
• Long Beach Boardwalk
• Sailors Haven, Fire Island
• Robert Moses State Park
• Sunken Meadow State Park

Jones Beach State Park

1 Ocean Parkway, Wantagh
Nassau, Town of Hempstead
516-785-1600
http://nysparks.state.ny.us, click on 'state parks'

Activities: Over a mile of **boardwalk** along a broad, sandy beach; **playground** and calm, shallow waters for wading tots at **Zach's Bay (Field 5)**.

Age: Interesting exhibits and activities for toddlers at the Theodore Roosevelt Nature Center; see Chapter 4, Indoor Escapes, for complete review.

Timing: Parking **Field 6** open year-round, daily, sunrise to sunset, other fields depend on season; **Zach's Bay generally only open weekends** during summer season; beaches can get packed on nice summer days - arrive as early as possible to minimize the walk from the parking lot. Nature center open weekends, 10-4pm.

Fees: Vehicle fee $8; no charge evenings, off-season and with Empire Passport sticker.

Finding It: Northern State Pkwy to the Meadowbrook *or* Wantagh Pkwy; take either road to the end and follow signs to Jones Beach and/or Ocean Pkwy.

Parking: For *Zach's Bay*, follow signs to **Field 5**. For *shortest beach & boardwalk access*, park at **Field 6**. For *Nature Center*, drive to the "West End" and follow signs for nature center.

Stroller: Boardwalk makes beach stroller–accessible.

Bathrooms: Diaper changing surfaces in ladies rooms. Restrooms open year-round at Field 6 only.

43

Food: Snack bars serve basic lunch food in season at
                   Zach's Bay, Field 6, and other parking fields. No
                   food at nature center, but there are picnic tables.

Jones Beach State Park is made up of several beaches, each
with its own distinct character and parking area. If you're driving
there, the first thing you need to decide is where to park. Here's a
quick lay of the land to help you determine the best spot for your
family.

Field 5,   Calm beach on **bay side**, preferred by young
Zach's Bay   **families** who can let **toddlers wade** in the
                   shallow water. The fenced-in **playground** is a
                   plus too but you'll miss the essence of the Jones
                   Beach experience which is on the Atlantic side:
                   crowds, rolling surf, and wide swaths of sand.

Fields 2,3,4   **Party on!** The beach here is swarming with
                   groups of string bikini-clad gals and hunky dudes
                   who keep the **Central Mall** hopping. You can
                   access the **boardwalk** here though, and the
                   waves are wild and wonderful, that is, once you
                   get past the patchwork quilt of beach blankets.

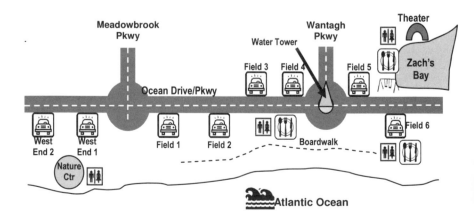

Field 6   A **mellow** alternative to the Central Mall area, the beach at Field 6 is favored by families with **lots of cargo**. Here you can **park just steps away from the sand**, provided you arrive early enough to get one of those coveted spots. You can also catch the **boardwalk** here and take baby for a long stroller ride.

West End   A more remote section of the park made for **nature lovers**. Unspoiled **dune ecosystems** thrive here, and although it's a bit too far off the beaten path for some, the chances of hearing a **bird song** here are much greater than that of a boom box.

Let's make a playdate! Meet at the Zach's Bay playground (under the Gazebo).

Theodore Roosevelt Nature Center

During the summer months, the nature center offers a convenient nearby shelter if you happen to be caught at **Jones Beach** in a downpour. Toddlers on up will enjoy the interesting **marine exhibits** and activities. *Outdoors* is a 1/3 mile-long boardwalk that makes a loop through a dune ecosystem which is short enough for toddler to walk without clamoring to be picked up.

Located at the "West End" of Jones Beach.
Generally open weekends, year-round, 10-4pm.
Call to confirm, 516-679-7254.

Long Beach Boardwalk

City of Long Beach
Nassau, Just south of the Town of Hempstead
516-431-1000
www.longbeachny.org, click on 'Summer Information'

Activities: 2 mile **boardwalk** along the ocean, cute toddler **playground**, wide sandy beach.

Timing: Boardwalk always accessible; boardwalk restaurant open for summer season only.

Fees: None for boardwalk; fee charged for beach in summer season: adults & children, $10; under 13, free. Day passes can be purchased on boardwalk at Long Beach & Edwards Blvd. or at beach entrance on National Blvd.

Finding it: Take Northern State Pkwy to Meadowbrook Pkwy south; take exit M10 onto Loop Pkwy; follow Loop Pkwy to end and turn right onto Lido Blvd. Go almost 4 miles - Lido Blvd will turn into Park Ave. Cross Long Beach Blvd and make next left onto Riverside Blvd. Go to last street (Broadway) and drive to desired boardwalk access point. (Riverside, National & Magnolia Blvd all have ramps leading up to boardwalk).

Parking: Lots of **free municipal parking** all along boardwalk, but occasionally challenging to get a spot on nice summer weekends. Weekdays are no problem though. Park at **Riverside** to be near bathrooms, **National** for snack bar, or at **Magnolia** to be near playground.

Stroller: Terrific, park and stroll up access ramp right onto boardwalk; no steps to negotiate.

Bathrooms: Public restroom located on boardwalk at **Riverside Blvd**; beach restrooms open during summer high season, no diaper changing tables but easy to improvise at numerous benches along boardwalk.

Food: Restaurant & snack bar right on boardwalk between Edwards & National Blvd - open late May to Labor Day, 10am-10pm, 516-431-0100. Several restaurants and diners along Park Ave across from the train station.

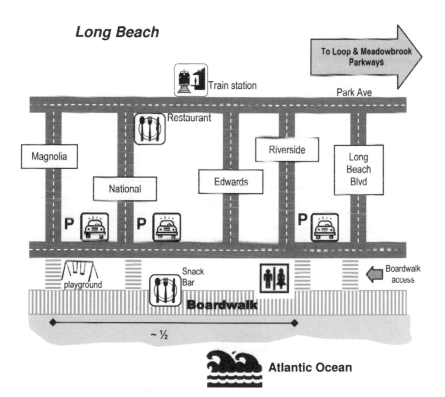

Long Beach

Atlantic Ocean

The Scoop:

You can stroll to your heart's content along this smooth, well-maintained **boardwalk that spans two miles of ocean front** in **Long Beach**. On a warm sunny day, you're bound to spot a virtual parade of strollers being vigorously pushed by moms burning off all that pregnancy flab. **Biker babies** are welcome as well, in a specially designated lane that keeps the flow of traffic orderly and safe.

After working up a sweat, you can give the little one a turn to romp at the adorable **playground** at Magnolia Boulevard that's designed especially for "1 somethings." In summer you can cruise down to the **snack bar** conveniently located right on the boardwalk. Serving up basics like chicken fingers, pizza, and burgers, it's nothing to write home about, but it does offer one of the only places to find **shade** along the beach.

Although the **waves might be a bit too choppy** for your small aspiring swimmer, the beach itself offers plenty of soft sand to wiggle baby's toes in. In July and August you have to pay $6 for the privilege of sitting on the sand. But at least then the many beach bathrooms are likely to be open – all the doors seem to be locked shut well into late June whenever I have visited.

A slave to creature comforts, I would have preferred if the public bathrooms, playground, boardwalk access, and beach ticket booth were all in one spot. Unfortunately such amenities are **spread out over about ½ a mile**, but then again the whole purpose is to get some **exercise**!

Sailors Haven, Fire Island

Ferry Leaves from Sayville
Suffolk, Town of Islip
Visitor Center 631-597-6183
www.nps.gov/fiis

Activities: Ferry ride to the Island, beautiful beach in natural setting; stroller-accessible, nature trails.

Age: Shady boardwalks through the forest seem magical to toddlers. But exercise caution - parts of boardwalk lack railings and even though it's not far to fall, there's poison ivy and deer ticks around.

Timing: **Seasonal.** The ferry is the only way to reach Sailors Haven and runs from mid-May to mid-Sept; call or log on for current schedule.

Duration: At least 3 hours with ferry ride.

Fees: Parking, $9, roundtrip ferry prices; adults, $12; children incl. babies, $7; no fee charged on Fire Island.

Finding It: LIE to exit 59S, follow Ocean Ave/Rte 93 south for a few miles, staying to the right as Rte 93 changes into Lakeland Ave. Continue through light intersection of Main St in Sayville and follow green signs for ferry.
From South: Sunrise Hwy (27) to exit 49, follow Lakeland Ave south, cross Main St (light intersection) and follow green signs for ferry.

Parking: Parking lot across the street from ferry terminal.

Ferry Info:

Sayville Ferry Service, 41 River Rd,
runs mid-May to mid-Sept., call or log on
for schedule.
631-589-8980
www.sayvilleferry.com
Ride lasts ~½ hour, ferry leaves promptly,
arrive at least 15 minutes early.

Stroller: Terrific! The abundance of boardwalks and
paved paths makes this is a stroller paradise.
Just a few steps required to get on and off ferry.

Food: Snack bar & grill; call visitor center for hours.

Bathrooms: Diaper changing table in ladies bathroom.

The Scoop:

A narrow strip of sand and soil that bisects the Great South Bay and even greater Atlantic Ocean, **Fire Island** is well known for its summer beach communities. But the island also lays claim to one of the most **pristine and unspoiled dune ecosystems** in the area, **the Sunken Forest**. And although the only way to reach this emerald jewel is by **ferry** (to **Sailors Haven**), the short boat ride is very enjoyable and an important part of the adventure for baby.

Operated by the National Park Service, the beaches at **Sailors Haven** offer a **breezy refuge** from the everyday stresses of the mainland. You and baby can relax in the natural surroundings but at the same time enjoy modern conveniences like diaper changing tables, picnicking facilities, and a snack bar. There is also a **visitor center** with a handful of **environmentally oriented exhibits**. And the best part is, it's all **stroller-accessible!**

Just steps from the ferry begins the **boardwalk trail** that loops around the Sunken Forest. The shaded paths meander past freshwater bogs, gently sloping dunes, and scrubby, maritime woodlands. And if you want to show toddler the difference between a Black Oak and a Tupelo tree, pick up a free guide to the plant life at the **visitor center.**

For a bit of cardiovascular training, you and hubby can take turns pushing the stroller all the way to the eastern limits of **Sailors Haven**. A brisk 15 minute walk will bring you to the end of the boardwalk and a series of fences marking the border with Cherry Grove, a lively gay and lesbian community.

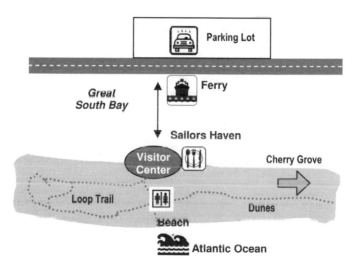

But if being a **beach bum** is your calling for the day, it's hardly a **five minute walk** from the ferry to the sand which is a good thing since you'll be schlepping all your cargo. Also keep in mind that there's **no natural shade** to speak of on the beach, so umbrellas and other sun-blockers come in handy.

Robert Moses State Park

Robert Moses Causeway, Babylon
Suffolk, Town of Babylon
www.nysparks.state.ny.us, click on 'State Parks"
631-669-0470

Activities: Wide, sandy beach, playground, about a mile of boardwalks for stroller rides.

Toddlers: Great playground at **Field 5**; good chance of spotting a **deer** along the lighthouse boardwalk.

Timing: Field 5 open year-round, daily, sunrise to sunset.

Fees: Vehicle fee $8; free off-season, evenings *or* with Empire Passport sticker.

Finding It: LIE Exit 53S, go south on Sagtikos Pkwy to Robert Moses Causeway. Continue over several bridges to the end. When you reach the tower, bear left around circle to reach Field 5. Entrance on right side.
From South: Take Southern State Pkwy to exit 41S onto Robert Moses Causeway, and follow directions above.

Parking: Drive to Field 5 and park to right of the building for closest access to playground. Lot may fill up in peak season, arrive by 10am to ensure a spot. Off-season and evenings are no problem.

Stroller: Plenty of boardwalks or paved paths with access ramps leading to beach.

Bathrooms: Ladies room has a diaper changing surface.

Food: Snack bar serving burgers and other lunch basics open during summer season.

The Scoop:

The large, well-maintained **playground** right by the beach is fabulous and reason enough to make an annual pilgrimage to **Robert Moses State Park**. The climbing equipment caters to every age group and even though the throngs of summer sun-worshippers keep the **beach** humming, the playground tends to be surprisingly un-congested.

Let's make a playdate! Meet at the playground under the gazebo.

Fitness-minded new parents can take advantage of the **boardwalk that spans almost a mile of oceanfront** and terminates at the **lighthouse**. It's about a 1½ mile stroller ride roundtrip to the lighthouse, and the small **museum** at its base provides a convenient rest stop. There's also the option to climb the **182 steps to the top of the tower**, but the **42" minimum height** requirement precludes even the tallest of toddlers from attempting it.

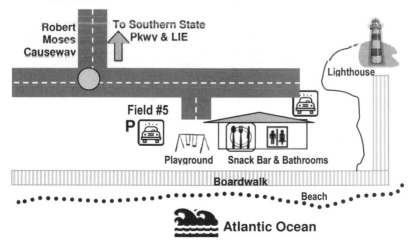

Sunken Meadow State Park

End of Sunken Meadow Parkway, Kings Park
Suffolk, Town of Smithtown
631-269-4333
www.nysparks.state.ny.us, click on 'State Parks"

Activities: Sandy beach, ¾ mile-long boardwalk,
playground at Parking Field 1.

Timing: Open year-round, sunrise to sunset; east end
snack bar open year-round, weekends 9-4pm
(also open weekdays during summer).

Fees: Vehicle fee $8; no charge off-season, after 4pm,
or with Empire Passport sticker.

Finding It: Exit 53 North off LIE, follow Sunken
Meadow/Sagtikos Pkwy to the end.

Parking: Parking lot at the eastern most end is closest to
snack bar that's open year-round and right next to
nature preserve.

Stroller: Great, boardwalk along beach and ramps from
parking lot to beach make it a convenient place to
take walks.

Food: **Snack bar** at main pavilion by Parking Field 1
open during summer season. Smaller snack bar
at eastern end of lot **serves food year-round on
weekends** and has casual indoor eating facilities.

Bathrooms: Public restrooms in both buildings – no diaper
changing tables but easy enough to wing it at the
beach.

The Scoop:

A long stretch of sandy beachfront along the pebble-ridden **North Shore**, Sunken Meadow State **Park** is a great place to build sand castles with a toddler. The nearly mile-long boardwalk also makes it an ideal spot to go for a bike ride with a baby, especially since there are many benches along the way to stop at, and enjoy the views.

As with all beachy hot spots, it's wise to bring sun protection - besides a few, sporadic gazebos and the umbrellas for rent in season, the park offers little respite from the rays. The **water tends to be pretty calm** though and you can splash around with small children without worrying about being engulfed by a tidal wave.

The beach at Sunken Meadow is part of an enormous park, and you'll pass several large, grassy picnic areas before you reach Parking Field 1 which services the main pavilion. In the heat of the summer, this concession is open daily, but como Fall it's more convenient to go all the way to the **last parking lot** where a smaller **snack bar serves food year-round on weekends.** Talk about waterfront dining in all seasons! There's no playground at this end but it does border a small but lovely **nature preserve** where you can take a short walk with toddler. And while some parents appreciate the **playground** near the main pavilion, I find its location by the parking lot a bit too far removed from the beach for my taste.

Tourist Towns

Feel like getting away from it all, and then making it home in time for dinner? Well hop on the expressway - fun tourist towns are just a few exits away!

If you're a local, you're probably familiar with the island's many **quaint villages** offering visitors plenty of **window shopping, sightseeing**, and **historic landmarks**. But when was the last time you visited? Between your job and the endless personal obligations tugging at you all these years, you may not have found the time to really get out there and explore it all. Well **now's your chance**; that recent addition to your household is the perfect excuse to **play tourist** and show baby the sights.

While there are scores of tourist destinations to choose from, the towns included in this section were selected for their **scenic appeal, convenient parking, stroller accessibility,** and child-friendly features such as **playgrounds, museums,** and other **points of interest** within easy walking distance from your car. Moderately-priced **restaurant recommendations** are included as well although budget-minded travelers can always pack a lunch from home.

Reviewed in This Section
• Northport Village
• Freeport Nautical Mile
• Great Neck Plaza
• Old Bethpage Restoration
• Sag Harbor Village
• Port Jefferson Village

Northport Village

Main and Woodbine Streets, Northport Village
Suffolk, Town of Huntington
www.northportny.com

Activities: Small, charming waterfront village lined with shops & restaurants, boat watching on the pier.

Toddlers: Wonderful sandy **playground** right on the harbor; second smaller playground in park across from pier; **farm animals** at the little barnyard down the road.

Timing: Any pleasant day when you're pining to be outdoors.

Finding It: *From East:* LIE exit 53N, Sunken Meadow Pkwy; take last exit for Rte 25A west, Huntington; follow 25A west approx 4½ miles. Cross over Waterside Rd and then bear right onto Main St. Go to end (intersection with Woodbine) and park. *From West:* Northern State Pkwy to exit 42N (Rte 231/Deer Park Ave north). Just past fire station bear right onto Deer Park Rd. Go about 1 mile and merge onto Rte 25, Jericho Tpke east. Get into left lane and make first left onto Elwood Rd. Continue on Elwood Rd for about 4 miles, crossing over Rte 25A where Elwood becomes Reservoir Ave then Church St. At intersection of Main St, make left. Go to end and park.

Parking: Free municipal lot by the harbor at intersection of Main St and Woodbine Ave.

Duration: 1-3 hours.

Stroller: Great; pier is also stroller-accessible.

Bathrooms: Public restrooms in Village Park (near intersection of Main & Woodbine by smaller playground) – no diaper changing tables.

Food: Numerous dining options along Main St. *For a partial view of the harbor try:* **Skipper's Pub,** 34 Main St, corner of Woodbine, 631-261-3589, www.skipperspub.com. Open daily from 11am; comfy booths, high chairs, crayons, strollers OK. *Or drive about a mile west to:* **The Shack**, 25A, just west of Northport on 25A in Centerport, 631-754-8989, www.theshack.org, completely outdoors, this casual seafood place is very popular in summertime.

The Scoop:

A picturesque little hamlet overlooking a boat-filled harbor, **Northport Village** evokes that pleasant old-town feel you might find in a Norman Rockwell painting. You can **start your walking tour at the pier** where the view of pleasure boats gliding by will immediately put you in a nautical state of mind. The **municipal lot** is right there as well and even though there's plenty of parking, it's worth **arriving early** on a nice day to secure a spot. Not that the village really ever gets packed, but on weekends you'll likely find the sidewalks **teeming with families (and strollers)**, perusing the shops and restaurants along **Main Street**.

The downtown is not huge; you'll likely cover the shopping district in less than an hour. But the **grassy park overlooking the harbor** is lovely and if you happen to be with a toddler, beware! The **playground** is irresistible and once my toddler got in there, it was virtually impossible to get him out. Fortunately it's **right on the water**, and completely enclosed, so you can allow your eyes to wander to the virtual parade of boats cruising along while she plays.

58

Northport Village

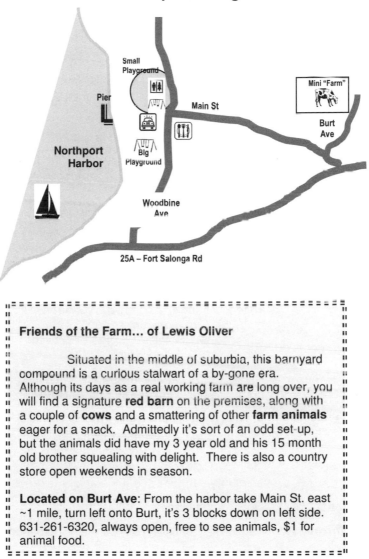

Friends of the Farm... of Lewis Oliver

Situated in the middle of suburbia, this barnyard compound is a curious stalwart of a by-gone era. Although its days as a real working farm are long over, you will find a signature **red barn** on the premises, along with a couple of **cows** and a smattering of other **farm animals** eager for a snack. Admittedly it's sort of an odd set-up, but the animals did have my 3 year old and his 15 month old brother squealing with delight. There is also a country store open weekends in season.

Located on Burt Ave: From the harbor take Main St. east ~1 mile, turn left onto Burt, it's 3 blocks down on left side. 631-261-6320, always open, free to see animals, $1 for animal food.

Freeport Nautical Mile

Woodcleft Avenue, Freeport
Nassau, Town of Hempstead
www.exploreli.com/entertainment/localguide/ click on South Shore
Nassau for list of restaurants

Activities: Stroller-friendly "Nautical Mile" lined with tourist shops and waterfront restaurants. Boat watching along the canal.

Timing: Lively, festive atmosphere in warmer months; I found the place a bit too desolate to visit in cold or rainy weather though; better to go sometime after noon when shops & restaurants are open.

Duration: 1-3 hours.

Finding It: Northern State Pkwy to Meadowbrook Pkwy. Take Meadowbrook South to exit M8W (Sunrise Hwy/Rte 27); follow Sunrise west about 0.8 mile. Turn left onto Guy Lombardo Ave (it's a traffic light intersection); go approx. 1 mile passing signs for waterfront area. Just after you see Randall Park on right, turn right onto Front St; make 1st quick left onto Woodcleft Ave; this begins the "Nautical Mile."

Playground: Randall Park (on Front Street & Guy Lombardo Ave-beginning of Nautical Mile).

Parking: Plenty of free street parking in early afternoon; free municipal lot about 1/3 way down Woodcleft on right. Otto's and Schooner restaurants have their own lots for customers; tougher to find a spot on balmy summer evenings and weekends.

Stroller: Good, ample sidewalks for strolling.

Bathrooms: Public restrooms at Randall Park in season and at end of mile by The Schooner restaurant.

Food: *Otto's Sea Grill*, 271 Woodcleft Ave, (about 2/3 way down the "mile" on left), 516-378-9480, *features:* dockside dining indoors or outdoors, stroller-friendly, kid's menu.

The Schooner, 435 Woodcleft Ave, at very end of Nautical Mile; www.theschooner.com, 516-378-7575; bay views, family-friendly.

Ralph's Italian Ices: 147A Woodcleft Ave, 516-771-2805.

The Scoop:

Parents seeking a change of scenery need look no further than Freeport's Nautical Mile. Little ones and their adult caregivers alike are sure to enjoy a leisurely afternoon at this "quaint cum kitschy" waterfront with its boats, fish markets and restaurants. Here you can take your time, and stop and smell the "fishes" – which is a good or bad thing, depending on your perspective.

But when it's a pleasant summer day and you feel like taking baby for a stroller ride, the **"Nautical Mile"** presents a novel alternative to the local park. There are plenty of points along the way where you can **watch boats glide** by along the adjacent canal, and there's a **small waterfront esplanade** with benches to sit at. You might even get a glimpse of a commercial fishing boat hauling in the **catch of the day**, ready to be grilled, sautéed or blackened to order at one of the seafood restaurants offering **dockside dining along the canal**.

Landlubbers can bide their time browsing the **tourist shops**, but for dessert everyone should indulge in a **Mai Tai, Strawberry Margarita**, or one of the many other **exotic-flavored frozen treats** at **Ralph's Famous Italian Ices**, located right on the Nautical Mile.

Great Neck Plaza

Middle Neck Road and Bond Street, Great Neck
Nassau, Town of North Hempstead
www.greatneckplaza.net

Activities: Vibrant downtown shopping district to explore, people watching, cafes; walking distance to nice public park with toddler playground.

Timing: Any time of year, as weather permits.

Duration: 1-3 hours, longer for shop-a-holics.

Finding It: LIE to exit 33, Lakeville Rd. Head north on Lakeville Rd crossing over Northern Blvd (25A) until it changes to Middle Neck Rd. Shopping area begins just past LIRR train station on right. City center at Grace Ave and Middle Neck Rd.

Parking: To be near playground, public bathrooms and restaurants, try municipal lot on corner of Grace Ave & Park St, across the street from the park. Tons of lots around but parking still can get tight on nice days.

Stroller: Terrific, strollers welcome in most stores and restaurants.

Bathrooms: Park restroom has diaper changing table.

Food: *Many restaurants to choose from; one longstanding favorite with the locals is:* **Pancho's Border Grill,** 10 Grace Ave, (between Middle Neck Rd & Bond St), 516-829-5305, www.panchostexmex.com, kid's menu, high chairs, changing tables, crayons.

The Scoop:

Besides being a **shopping paradise** for fashionistas of all stripes, polka dots, and plaids, **Great Neck Plaza** deserves the grand prize for diaper-changing facilities. Many restaurants have them as do the **public restrooms in the town park**.

On temperate days, **scores of strollers** inhabit the sidewalks of this bustling downtown area. And what "the Plaza" lacks in quaint, historical charm (like some of the other towns reviewed in this section), is compensated for by its endless shopping opportunities. **Feel like reviving your wardrobe?** The window displays are dripping with chic shoes and apparel catering to all kinds of tastes and design sensibilities. If it's your first time here though, prepare yourself for sticker shock the prices can verge on obscene. But then again, it doesn't cost anything to look.

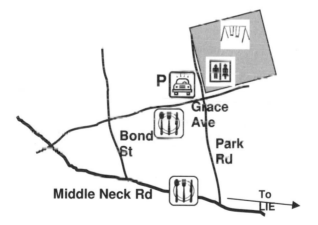

When the little one wants a little action, a **good toddler playground** is close by, and if you're fortunate enough to score a parking spot in the municipal lot across the street from it, you can have shops, **baby-friendly dining**, and a playground all within a **five minute walking radius**.

Old Bethpage Village Restoration

Round Swamp Road, Old Bethpage
Nassau, Town of Oyster Bay
516-572-8400/1

Activities: Historic buildings of adult interest.

Age: Infants on up.

Toddlers: Wonderful open spaces for toddler to explore; live animals in farm area; toddlers welcome in historic buildings but there are steps and roped-off areas to steer them clear of.

Timing: Open March through December; hours vary but generally Wed-Sun, 10-4pm; log on or call to find out about special events, it's more crowded on those days but there's also more to do.

Duration: 2-4 hours.

Fees: Adults, $10; children over 4, $7; under 5, free.

Finding It: **From West:** LIE east to exit 48; turn right onto Round Swamp Rd; at light turn left and you'll see entrance on left.
From East: LIE west to exit 48. Make left onto Round Swamp Rd. Go approx. 1 mile through underpass; go left at next light to entrance.

Parking: Good if you **arrive early** and get a spot right by the entrance but lot can fill up fast.

Stroller: Access to historic village requires long stroller ride on gravel paths. Since some buildings are not stroller-accessible, it may be easier to transport infants with a baby carrier. You'll probably want the stroller as well, even for late-stage toddlers, to cover extensive grounds.

Bathrooms: Visitor Center ladies room has diaper changing tables, additional bathrooms on grounds.

Food: Generally no food or drink served unless there's a special event; you can bring food to eat at their designated indoor/outdoor dining areas.

The Scoop:

From the parking lot, plan on walking about ten minutes before reaching the first historic site at **Old Bethpage Village Restoration**. Dating back to the **Civil War**, the buildings have been painstakingly restored to re-create a village replete with a **general store, school, church** and even a **saloon** that occasionally serves root beer to thirsty visitors. The place is also teeming with friendly folks dressed in period costume who manage to bring this 19th century village to life.

Throughout the season, **special events** are held in the village, many of interest to both adults and children. We happened to be there for "Hands-on Saturday," and enjoyed a round of **bean bag toss** and other games played by children before the age of Nintendo. A little further down was a **farm with sheep, cows, and two huge hogs**. On many weekends, you can also watch a **baseball game** there, played according to the rules back in 1867. Bring sun block though, I have no idea if they used it back then, but it's good to have some protection on the **un-shaded paths**.

65

Sag Harbor Village

Main Street, Sag Harbor
Suffolk, Town of Southampton
Village Info: 631-725-0222
www.sagharborchamber.com

Activities: Charming seaside village with shops, gourmet restaurants, and historic buildings. For children: puppet theater, beach with small playground, large playground at nearby Mashashimuet Park, children's section of Bookhampton Book Store.

Timing: Better to coordinate trip with a visit to the Puppet Theater. In general, July and August are the busiest months. **June and Sept** are great months to visit because it's still warm, less crowded, and there's **no charge at Haven's Beach**.

Duration: Couple hours to a whole day.

Finding It: LIE to exit 70 (Manorville); head south on Rte 111 for approx. 4½ miles following signs for Rte 27 (Sunrise Hwy). Take Rte 27 east (which begins where Rte 111 ends). After approx. 16 miles, you'll see signs for "North Sea, Noyack Rd, Sag Harbor." At light, make soft left onto Rte 52 north. Bear left and follow Noyack Rd/North Sea signs. About 7 miles down Noyack Road on the left is entrance to the Elizabeth A. Morton Wildlife Refuge. Continue another 2 miles, make left at the circle and drive along Long Beach. Continue for about 2 more miles and make right onto Rte 114 south. Cross over bridge, make right onto Main St and look for parking in Sag Harbor Village. Note: back-tracking on the way home is a bit tricky as the road names seem to constantly change.

For **Puppet Theater** take Main St about ¾ mile, and make **left onto Union St.** (Note the **Whaling Museum** on right side at 200 Main St - it's a big white Greek Revival House with tall columns). Follow Union St a few blocks to intersection with Division & Rte 114. (Christ Episcopal **Church** will be on the corner). Cross over to E. Union and look for theater on **right side.** Next door to church, across from school.

Parking: Lots of free street parking and municipal lots; parking a bit tight in July & August but doable.

Stroller: Terrific, plenty of sidewalks.

Food: For comprehensive list of restaurants, see www.sagharborchamber.com and click on restaurants. One suggestion...
Conca D'Oro Pizzaria Restaurant, 103 Main St, 631-725-3167, very casual pizza place, kid-friendly.

Bathrooms: Public bathrooms with diaper changing table in little gray house on **Bay St** near the wharf (across from the intersection of Division St).

The Scoop:

Nestled between the North and South forks of Long Island, the former **whaling port of Sag Harbor** is now a very popular tourist destination in summer. Find a parking spot in town and you're within walking distance to **shops, restaurants, a scenic wharf** with an authentic **windmill,** and the wonderful **Goat on a Boat Puppet Theater.**

History aficionados will discover more than a dozen churches and homes, some dating as far back as the mid-18th century. Vestiges of their maritime past can still be found in the architecture, and in the stately building occupied by the **Whaling Museum,** (which was also once the residence of a prominent **whale ship owner**).

67

For my toddler though, the highlight of our visit was the **"playgroup"** at the Puppet Theater. Held mostly in the mornings, these interactive puppet encounters are a great way to begin a daytrip to Sag Harbor. Afterwards, you can head outdoors to the **calm waters** of **Haven's Beach.** Although a parking fee is collected from out-of-towners in July and August, the beach does provide a sheltered place for little ones to splash about freely, and the little **playground** right on the sand is an added bonus.

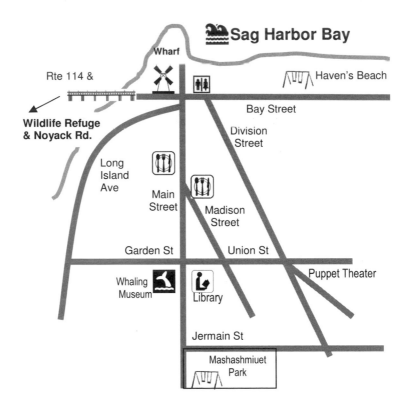

Fun Stuff in Sag Harbor

Sag Harbor Whaling Museum
200 Main St.
Complete review in Chapter 4 – Indoor Escapes

Haven's Beach
Entrance near 143 **Bay St** (between Hempstead & Prospect St).
Basic playground, gazebo with picnic tables, calm water for tots to
wade in. Beach fee charged July & Aug, all other times free.

Goat on a Boat Puppet Theater
Rtc 114 & E. Union St.
*Complete review in
Chapter 4 – Indoor Escapes*

Bookhampton Book Store
20 Main St, 631-725-8425.
Book store with cute children's section.

Mashashimuet Park
Jermain & Main St.
Extensive playground about a mile
from village center.

Slightly Off the Beaten Path

Elizabeth A. Morton National Wildlife Refuge
Noyack Rd (4 miles from Sag Harbor Village), 631-286-0485.
Open daily, sunrise to sunset, $4 vehicle fee, bathrooms on site.
A ¾ **mile nature trail** along a pebbly, but stroller-accessible path
passes through verdant landscapes and concludes at a pristine
stretch of **sandy beach** with lovely views of the bay.
www.fws.gov/northeast/longislandrefuges/morton.html

Port Jefferson Village

Main Street (25A) in Port Jefferson Village
Suffolk, Town of Brookhaven
www.portjeffchamber.com

Activities: Window-shopping, waterfront dining, ferry rides in season. Playground, children's museum, public library is right in the village and has a nice children's section.

Duration: 2-4 hours.

Finding It: LIE to exit 64; head north on Rte 112 (Port Jefferson and Patchogue Rd) for about 8-9 miles until you reach Port Jefferson. When Rte 112 turns into Main St, start looking for signs for parking lots.

Parking: Several municipal lots with free parking; check the lots behind the Harbor Square Mall to be near playground. Enter from Maple or Wynn St.

Stroller: Terrific; a popular place for strollers.

Food: Many restaurants to choose from. Website for Port Jefferson Chamber of Commerce has a list of restaurants. www.portjeffchamber.com. Here is one with a view:
Steam Room, 4 East Broadway, across street from ferry terminal. *Features:* Casual, order food at counter, high chairs, strollers OK, no diaper changing table. 631-928-6690, ww.steamroomportjefferson.com.

Bathrooms: Public restrooms inside Harbor Square Mall, library and ferry terminal. The library and ferry terminal bathrooms have diaper changing units.

The Scoop:

Surrounding a scenic harbor, **Port Jefferson Village** is a magnet for tourists in pleasant weather. It's no wonder why; the charming, historic streets are lined with **shops and restaurants.** This lovely seaside town also offers a multitude of activities to try with small children. If it's really nice out, you can hop aboard the ferry or even a "paddle cruiser" for a tour of the Long Island Sound.

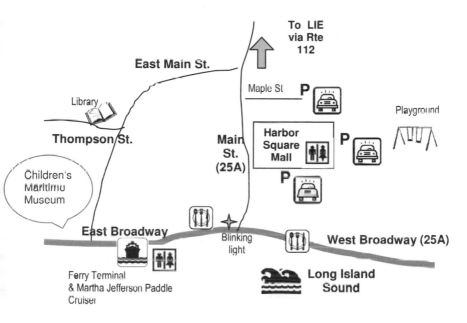

To explore the town by foot, start at the harbor, (by the **blinking light** across from the **ferry terminal),** and saunter up Main Street (25A). A few blocks further, turn left onto *East* Main Street, where you will spot a number of quaint historic homes. Some more uphill stroller-pushing will strengthen your biceps and bring you to the entrance of the **public library** which has a nice children's section and a restroom with a diaper changing table. You can stop there, or continue back down the hill to the water and complete the loop.

If the weather takes a turn for the worse, take a stroll over to the Children's Maritime Museum. Overlooking the harbor by a lovely waterfront park, the museum's small space has an impressive array of toys and activities for little ones.

Things to Do in Port Jefferson Village:

Children's Maritime Museum (reviewed in Ch. 4)
101-A East Broadway,
(just a couple blocks past Ferry Terminal),
631-331-3277,
www.childrensmaritimemuseum.org.

Port Jefferson Steamboat Ferry
631-473-0286,
www.bpjferry.com,
scenic ferry ride across the Sound to Bridgeport,
about three hours roundtrip.
Check website for current schedule.
Adults, $18.50 R/T, children under 5, free.

Martha Jefferson Paddle Cruiser
One hour sightseeing tour,
runs daily in July & August, $8 for adults; $4 kids.
Port Jefferson Harbor,
631-331-3333,
www.marthajefferson.com.

Public Library
100 Thompson St, corner of East Main St,
red phone booth on the corner.
631-473-0022,
http://pjfl.suffolk.lib.ny.us.

4

Indoor Escapes

It's Raining, It's Pouring...

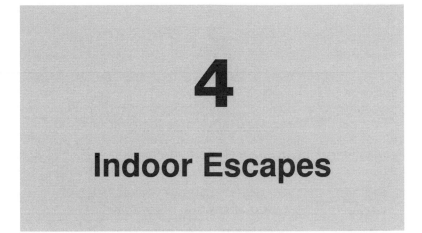

It seems like there are plenty of things to do when it's warm and sunny, but when the **winter doldrums** set in, the desire to nest at home becomes strong. If you're anything like me though, you know you'll go crazy hanging around the house, and one more trip to the mall may spell the end of your credit card limit!

Well forget about shopping for awhile! A whole smorgasbord of **indoor entertainment** options awaits little ones and their caregivers, be they **moms, dads, grandmas, or nannies**. The pages of this chapter are filled with all kinds of **fun, interesting, and *unusual*** places to check out with the kiddies. And the best part is that most of them lend themselves to spontaneous, **spur-of-the-moment visits** where you can drop in, pay, and hang out in a climate controlled environment. So slip on those galoshes, grab the umbrella, and don't forget to **call before you go** to ensure they are open and running on schedule.

I Spy .... A Museum

Looking for a bit of **intellectual stimulation** between episodes of Barney and Sesame Street? How about visiting a museum? Increasingly catering to younger clientele, many museums offer **hands-on, interactive learning opportunities** for toddlers to enjoy. It's a fun way to learn about **art, science, and history**, and many museums hold special programs and events as well, that are suitable **for the whole family**.

Reviewed in This Section

- Cold Spring Harbor Whaling Museum
- Cradle of Aviation
- Garvies Point Museum
- Heckscher Museum of Art
- Long Island Children's Museum
- Long Island Museum of Art, History & Carriages
- Nassau County Museum of Art
- Sag Harbor Whaling Museum
- Children's Museum of the East End
- Children's Maritime Museum

Don't expect anything on the scale or sophistication of the Museum of Natural History in Manhattan though. Rather, think of Long Island museums as **compact spaces** to hang out in when it's miserable outside.

> Visit Tip: Make it a game of search and find. Walking around the space and playing "I Spy" makes even the driest exhibits interesting for little ones.

While some of the places reviewed in this section have excellent exhibits, others consist of no more than a couple rooms with fairly basic display cases. But then again, toddlers won't know the difference, and guaranteed they'll go home having learned something new about the world.

Cold Spring Harbor Whaling Museum

Main Street (also 25A), Cold Spring Harbor, Suffolk
631-367-3418, www.cshwhalingmuseum.org

Activities: Historic artifacts, children's room with activities.

Age: Stroller babies on up; easy to keep track of toddler in compact space; sturdy exhibits.

Timing: Tue-Sun, 11-5pm, it gets crowded with school groups, call ahead if you wish to avoid them.

Duration: An hour tops.

Fees: Adults, $5; children under 5, free; $4, ages 5-18.

Finding It: LIE to Rte 106 north; take Rte 106 ~4 miles; turn right at light onto Northern Blvd (25A); go ~5 miles on 25A. Pass village of Cold Spring Harbor, museum will be white building on left.

Parking: Usually plenty of street parking right by entrance.

Stroller: Completely stroller-accessible.

Bathrooms: No diaper changing facilities in the restrooms.

Food: Not permitted – OK to feed baby a bottle; several cafes within a five minute walk down the street in Cold Spring Harbor Village.

The Scoop:

This small but quaint museum is laden with whaling artifacts. It has a reproduction whaling ship bed to climb onto, and your little Sea Captain can have a go at a ship's steering wheel. The children's room, with its puzzles, games, puppets, and crayons will also keep them busy for awhile. Though the museum is too small to warrant a trip from afar, it can be combined with a visit to the nearby **Fish Hatchery** (reviewed in Chapter 3) and a saunter through historic **Cold Spring Harbor Village** for a half day of educational fun.

Cradle of Aviation Museum

Charles Lindbergh Boulevard, Garden City
Nassau, Town of Hempstead
516-572-4111
www.cradleofaviation.org

Activities: Huge space with life-size planes and other exhibits of interest to both toddlers and adults.

Age: Stroller babies and up; adults will enjoy it and infants can come along for the ride; terrific for young children though you may have to block toddlers from running into large open exhibits that are cordoned off by only a velvet rope.

Timing: Open 9:30-5:00pm, Tues-Sun. Open every day in summertime. Café open 10-4pm.

Duration: An hour or a whole afternoon.

Fees: Adults, $9; children over 2, $8; under 2, free.

Finding It: Take Southern State Pkwy or Northern State Pkwy to Meadowbrook Parkway. Take exit M4, follow signs to Museum Row, proceed onto Charles Lindbergh Blvd, at 2nd light, turn right into parking lot.

Parking: Large lot.

Stroller: Very good; baby can remain in stroller the whole time; second floor accessible by elevator.

Bathrooms: Changing tables in the ladies room.

Food: Light lunches served at the spacious Red Planet Café; no outside food allowed but OK to bring snacks/drinks for children, hot water available to warm baby's bottle.

The Scoop:

Young children seem to enjoy this **"airplane museum,"** which from their vantage point, is a **gigantic indoor space** filled with all sorts of strange, winged objects. Grown-ups however, will find an interesting survey of the history and future of air travel. And flat, wide-open space is perfect for wheeling around a stroller.

While the exhibits at the Cradle of Aviation are truly first class, (pun intended), I did find it challenging to take it all in while keeping my roaming child in check. Many of the planes on display are cordoned off with rope which means nothing to a toddler. So I just chased mine around until he finally discovered the **"cockpits"** which he could climb into and play **pretend pilot**. There is also a special children's area with hands-on activities that cater to the five and under crowd.

Let's make a playdate! Meet inside the Red Planet Cafe

The **Cradle of Aviation** is terrific and **worth making a daytrip** for, even from the far reaches of Suffolk County. Within the building is also the Nassau County Firefighters Museum which can be accessed for an additional fee. It has several interactive exhibits including a section for children to dress up as firefighters, but doesn't take long to go through.

Right next door is the equally wonderful **Children's Museum** and it's easy to spend a whole day between the two places. Folks living in Nassau may prefer to visit them on two separate occasions though to avoid getting "museumed-out." I love going to museums, but a couple hours of tailing a little one is usually enough to exhaust me.

Garvies Point Museum & Preserve

50 Barry Drive, Glen Cove
Nassau, Town of North Hempstead
516-571-8010/11
www.co.nassau.ny.us/parkmuse.html

Activities: Interesting exhibits for both toddlers & adults.

Age: Toddlers & up.

Toddlers: Very toddler-friendly; two rooms containing exhibits at toddler eye level; wigwam in the back is fun to crawl around in.

Timing: Open Tues-Sun, 10-4pm, year-round; it can feel crowded when school groups show up.

Duration: An hour or less.

Fees: Adults, $2; children, 4-14, $1; under 4, free.

Finding it: Exit 41N off LIE. Take Rte 107 North for several miles until the road seems to end in front of a fire station. Turn right onto Brewster, get in left lane and turn left at traffic light onto Cottage Rd. From there, follow brown signs for "N.C. Garvies Point Museum". It's several more turns through a residential neighborhood to the entrance.

Parking: Very good, dedicated parking lot near the entrance.

Stroller: Great-no steps, exhibit halls wide enough to accommodate strollers.

Bathrooms: Fold-out diaper changing unit in ladies room.

Food: None served but picnic tables outside and indoor dining area to bring a bagged lunch.

The Scoop:

The exhibits at this small **museum** chronicle the **geological and archeological history** of Long Island. And while at first glance it might not seem like much, take a little time to browse around with your child. Toddlers in particular seem to enjoy peeking into the glass cases displaying **Native American artifacts** and mine spent an inordinate amount of time studying the dioramas depicting scenes of the everyday lives of the **Indians** who lived here so many moons ago. But to access the exhibit hall, you have to first pass through the "gift shop gauntlet." My toddler found its diverse selection of nature-oriented books and toys completely enthralling, and it took a solid 15 minutes to wrench the sale items out of his hand before we were able to go see the main attraction.

 **Garvies Point Museum** is a surprisingly good place to meet for a **playdate.** The dining area in the back is pretty mellow (as long as a school group hasn't invaded), and you can sit at the tables and munch on home-brought snacks while the peewees explore the dug-out canoe and wigwam.

With toddler attention spans what they are, touring the interior will probably take under an hour. But if it's nice out, you can go for a walk on one of the trails in the surrounding **nature preserve** afterwards. Admittedly, I did find the bumpy paths a bit difficult to navigate with a stroller, but the woodland setting does provide a short and sweet **introduction to hiking** for strong toddlers.

As long as you're not expecting something on the scale and grandeur of the Museum of Natural History in Manhattan, you and the little one can certainly enjoy an interesting history lesson or two here. You may even want to return for their **Annual Thanksgiving Festival** which is fun and features many hands-on activities for children.

Heckscher Museum of Art

2 Prime Avenue, Huntington
Suffolk, Town of Huntington
631-351-3251
www.heckscher.org

Activities: Art viewing mainly of adult interest, though it's surprising what can spark a toddler's curiosity.

Age: Stroller babies and up; little ones with short attention spans may not last long unless you play "I Spy" and turn the act of looking at art into a game. Playground and duck pond in adjacent park.

Timing: Open Tue-Fri, 10-5pm, Sat & Sun, 1-5pm; better to visit weekdays when it's quieter and strollers aren't an issue.

Duration: 45 minutes or so.

Fees: Adults, $5; ages 6-12, $1; under 5, free.

Finding It: LIE to exit 49S; follow Rte 110 south for about 6 miles (road changes name to NY Ave). Turn right at light onto 25A/ Main St. Make left onto Prime Ave (light). Museum parking lot on right.

Parking: Very good; parking lot right by the entrance.

Stroller: Entrance and gallery space are stroller accessible; bathrooms down a flight of steps.

Bathrooms: No diaper changing facilities in restrooms.

Food: None permitted or served; benches outside in park to eat a bag lunch; or dine in nearby Huntington Village; *Mundays* at 259 Main St. is kid-friendly, 631-421-3553.

The Scoop:

"Look mommy! A fire truck!" Well those certainly weren't the words I expected to hear from my toddler in an *art* museum. But sure enough, an image of a racing red engine adorned the walls along with taxicabs, subway cars, and garbage trucks, all part of an exhibition of the artist, Red Grooms. Never heard of him? That's not unusual at the **Heckscher Museum of Art** which often showcases very talented, yet lesser known artists.

Regardless of who is featured at their frequently **changing exhibits,** you can always find imaginative depictions of "people, places, and things" to observe with baby. **Weekdays** tend to be pretty mellow and little ones can enjoy an unobstructed view of the art from their stroller. When it's busy though, four wheelers aren't quite as welcome, as they are seen as a hindrance to fellow art patrons.

Admittedly the gallery space is **pretty small** and adults will likely need no more than an hour to get their fill. Young children might get restless sooner though, and even though my toddler happened to appreciate the subject matter at that particular exhibit, he was ready to split after about twenty minutes.

But maybe he was simply eager to get back outside and explore **Heckscher Park**, which begins a few steps from the museum entrance. It's easy to spend an afternoon there ambling over its sloping lawns, duck pond trail, and the recently revamped playground featuring equipment for children of all ages.

Long Island Children's Museum

11 Davis Avenue, Garden City
Nassau, Town of Hempstead
516-224-5800
www.licm.org

Activities: Excellent, hands-on exhibits; special play area for toddlers called "Tot Spot".

Age: Crawling babies on up; great place to bring the infant /toddler sibling combo.

Timing: July-Aug: daily, 10-5pm; Sept-June: Tuesday-Sunday, 10-5pm; better to go on weekdays or first thing on weekends to avoid the crowds.

Duration: 2-4 hours.

Fees: Adults & children over 1, $10; under 1 year, free.

Finding It: *From South:* Take Southern State Pkwy to Meadowbrook Pkwy north; take exit M4, following signs for Nassau Coliseum until you're on Charles Lindbergh Blvd. Go through light, entrance on right.
From North: Northern State Pkwy to Meadowbrook Pkwy south; take exit M4 & follow signs for Nassau Coliseum; after about ¼ mile, take right fork onto Charles Lindbergh Blvd. Continue to entrance on right.

Parking: Plenty of parking in the large lot.

Stroller: This place is practically a stroller showroom!

Bathrooms: Changing tables in the ladies & men's room; also a family restroom that fits the whole gang as well as the stroller.

Food: No food served, the cafeteria has a few vending machines with basic snacks, visitors can eat home-brought food; no place to warm baby's bottle though.

The Scoop:

A superb destination for creative exploration, the **Long Island Children's Museum** features hands-on, interactive exhibits that even appealed to **crawling babies** like my 11 month old son, Tycho.

Though we had mainly visited to entertain his big brother Ben, Tycho found a safe harbor to play at the **"TotSpot,"** a contained area with a pretend **grocery store, train, lighthouse, and fishing boat** complete with a conveyor belt to pull up lobsters. While Ben fiddled with the controls of a bright, yellow backhoo, Tycho and I sat in a corner playing with **hand puppets**. TotSpot is very popular though and they control the crowd by giving out **tickets designating the time you can go** at the admission counter. On weekends, the museum gets busy, and it's good to arrive as close to opening time as possible so you don't have to wait hours for your turn at TotSpot.

If you do have to wait though, time will fly as your toddler explores the rest of this spacious museum with its **bubbles, blocks, musical instruments**, and sand. It's a true multi-sensory experience, and I had almost as much fun as my little ones discovering all it had to offer. The museum is really **worth driving the distance** from eastern Suffolk and you can make a daytrip out of it if you bring lunch along.

Let's make a playdate! Meet in the cafeteria.

Long Island Museum
of Art, History & Carriages

1200 Route 25A, Stony Brook
Suffolk, Town of Brookhaven
631-751-0066
www.longislandmuseum.org

Activities: Exhibits of interest to both adults and children.

Age: Stroller-bound babies and up.

Toddler: Great wide open spaces for toddler to explore; exhibits are roped off, but curious toddlers may be tempted to trespass (mine was!)

Timing: Open Wed-Sat, 10-5pm, Sun, 12-5pm; call or log on to find out about children's programs.

Duration: 2-4 hours, or make a day trip out of it and enjoy lunch and a stroll in nearby Stony Brook Village (about 1/2 mile from museum).

Fees: Adults, $9; 6-17, $4; children under 6, free.

Finding It: LIE to exit 62; head north on Nicholls Rd/Rte 97 approx. 10 miles to the end. Turn left onto Rte 25A and continue for another 1-2 miles. At the 'T', make left onto Main St. Make first quick right into museum parking lot.

Parking: Very good; parking lot right by the entrance.

Stroller: Completely stroller-accessible and necessary even with good walkers to cover large grounds.

Food: None served, but you can bring your own food to eat at their outdoor picnic tables. Several restaurants about ½ mile east in the Village Green. Two to check out: The Brook House Restaurant, 631-751-3332, The Golden Pear Café, 631-751-7695, strollers OK.

| **Diapers:** | Bathrooms in every building but none with diaper changing facilities. I was told that there are plans to install a changing table soon though. If need be, the bathrooms in the Carriage Museum are large enough to spread a towel on the floor to change baby. |

The Scoop:

Filled with historic artifacts that shed light on the Island's storied past, the **Long Island Museum of American Art, History, and Carriages** is an interesting place to explore for parents and toddlers alike on a rainy afternoon. Bring galoshes though; the museum complex is actually comprised of **three separate buildings,** each about a three minute walk from the other.

Tickets to all the museums can be purchased at the **History Museum** which is just steps from the main parking lot. My toddler really enjoyed its **gallery of miniature rooms,** which were furnished with thumb-sized sofas, beds, and dining sets, many lit by miniscule, but real working light fixtures!

Let's make a playdate! Meet at the entrance to the History Museum.

With its extensive collection of colorful, horse-drawn carriages, **the Carriage Museum** across the street is also fun for youngsters. There was even a quaint reproduction of Stony Brook Village at the turn-of-the-century replete with a post office and general store.

Nassau County Museum of Art

One Museum Drive, Roslyn Harbor
Nassau, Town of North Hempstead
516-484-9338
www.nassaumuseum.com

Activities: Art, mainly of adult interest. Check website for outdoor festivals and children's programs.

Age: Stroller-bound babies and mellow toddlers; Tee Ridder collection of miniature rooms is good for a round of "I Spy" with children.

Timing: Open Tue-Sun, 11-5pm.

Duration: 1-2 hours.

Fees: Adults, $10; under 5, free (admission price includes Tee Ridder Miniature Museum); parking fee of $2 charged on weekends.

Finding It: LIE to exit 39N. Take Glen Cove Rd. north approx. 2 miles, turn left onto Northern Blvd (Rte 25A). At 2nd light, turn right into Museum Drive.

Parking: Parking lot is a 5 minute walk to museum which involves some steps along pathway.

Stroller: Museum is completely stroller-accessible; ask for elevator to the 2nd floor. Better to visit on quiet weekdays when it's easier to negotiate the narrow hallways and small rooms.

Bathrooms: Restroom on 2nd floor has a makeshift place to change diapers.

Food: Café on ground floor; OK to bring bottle and baby food into museum.

The Scoop:

For **art aficionados** seeking a little cultural diversion between diaper changes and bottle feedings, this **elegant pair of museums** offers a convenient alternative to schlepping into Manhattan. Even those who don't understand what the big deal is about Picasso anyway might enjoy getting out of the house to view **splashes of cheerful, bright color** on a drab, overcast day.

Or just go to tour the **stately mansion**, which was once actually a **wedding gift!** It was purchased in 1919 by the steel magnate, Henry Clay Frick for his soon to be betrothed son. That was life in the good old days, before taxes and regulation!

Today there are a number of playful modern sculptures gracing the lawns, and an adorable collection of **miniature furniture** at the **Tee Ridder Museum** which is also located on the property.

For me, the ideal time to go to adult-oriented museums was when my own little "masterpiece" was still an **infant** and content to view the art, or even snooze, from the comfort of his stroller. And though I had misgivings about bringing a baby to such a traditionally quiet place, I was glad to find the staff welcoming, and even a number of elderly visitors peeking into the stroller for a glimpse of my own newly-minted patron of the arts.

87

Sag Harbor Whaling Museum

200 Main Street, Sag Harbor
Suffolk, Town of Southampton
631-725-0770
www.sagharborwhalingmuseum.org

Activities: Whaling-related artifacts, mainly of adult interest.

Age: Stroller-bound babies on up.

Toddlers: Good for a short period; a few exhibits may pique toddler's interest but he or she probably won't last too long here. Gift shop has nautical-themed toys and picture books. Cute children's section in public library across street is a nice option.

Finding It: LIE to Exit 70 (Manorville); follow Rte **111** south for several miles and follow signs for Rte 27. When Rte 111 ends, road veers left and turns into Rte 27. Head east on **Rte 27** for about **23 miles**. Go through Village of **Bridgehampton** and make left at traffic light onto Sag Harbor Turnpike **(Rte 79)**. (Just before turn is a **sign for Shelter Island Ferry**). Continue on Rte 79 about 4 miles until road changes name to Main Street. The **Whaling Museum is on left side** at 200 Main St at the corner of Garden Street. It's a big white Greek Revival House with tall columns.

Timing: Open mid-May to late September, 10-5pm, Mon-Sat, 1-5pm, Sundays; open Oct-Dec weekends, 12-4pm. Call/check website to confirm hours.

Duration: Half an hour.

Fees: Adults, $5; children under 12, free.

Parking: Street parking on Main Street and some side streets; can get tricky in high season.

Stroller: A few steps to get into building; all exhibits on ground floor and are stroller-accessible.

Food: No food served or permitted on premises-for nearby dining options, see review of Sag Harbor Village in Chapter 3-Fair Weather Outings.

Bathrooms: No diaper changing facilities in the restrooms; public library across the street has diaper changing tables, only accessible by steps though.

The Scoop:

Adult **history buffs** will enjoy the diverse assortment of bric-a-brac dating back to the 1700s displayed in this impressive former residence of a whale ship owner. Besides the collection of **harpoons, ship parts** and other objects harkening back to the **whaling Industry,** the museum possesses a number of household artifacts Including some **early toy train sets** that my toddler couldn't understand why he wasn't allowed to play with.

Comprised of just a few rooms occupying the ground floor of the house, the museum can be **toured fairly quickly.** But its close proximity to Sag Harbor makes it a fun place to drop by for a quick visit on the way into town, and gain insight into the village's great whaling legacy.

Day-trippers take note:

A complete description of Sag Harbor Village and its offerings can be found in Chapter 3.

Children's Museum of the East End

376 Bridgehampton/Sag Harbor Turnpike, Bridgehampton
Suffolk, Town of Southampton
631-537-8250, www.cmee.org

Activities: Interactive exhibits, classes, special events.

Age: Crawlers on up, toddler programs for walkers on up to about 5 years.

Timing: Mon-Sat, 9-5pm; Sun, 10-5pm; closed Tue., or sign up for a special program like Toddler Tuesdays and schedule visit accordingly.

Duration: 1-2 hours.

Fees: General Admission, $7; under 1 year, free.

Finding It: LIE (495 East) to exit 70 Manorville. Follow Rte 111 to Rte 27 East (Sunrise Hwy) toward Montauk. Stay on Rte 27, past Southampton to Bridgehampton. Make left at monument in Bridgehampton onto Bridgehampton/Sag Harbor Turnpike (County Rd 79) and continue for ~0.5 miles. Museum is just past railroad tracks on left.

Stroller: Easy, park in the lot and stroll right in.

Bathrooms: Changing table in men's and ladies' room.

Food: Food and drinks OK in lobby but not in museum. Vending machines on site. Nearby restaurant: Candy Kitchen, Main St., 631-537-9885.

The Scoop:

The inviting, tastefully designed exhibits at this wonderful museum highlight favorite Hampton sights including a windmill, farm stand, and a lighthouse. Children can play at the quaint pretend soda fountain, and when they get the munchies, everyone can get a scoop of the real thing at the nearby Candy Kitchen, a classic luncheonette with a working soda fountain, that also happens to be very kid-friendly.

Children's Maritime Museum

101-A East Broadway, Port Jefferson, Suffolk
631-331-3277
www.childrensmaritimemuseum.org

Activities: Interactive, hands-on activities, drop-off summer programs for ages 4+.

Age: Toddlers on up, good for multi-aged siblings.

Timing: Sat & Sun, 1-5pm.

Duration: 1-2 hours.

Fees: $5 per person (adults & children).

Finding It: LIE to exit 62. Follow Rte 97 (Nicolls Road) north to end. Turn right onto Rte 25A east and follow into downtown Port Jefferson. Bear left at flashing light and proceed past ferry docks and Danford's Inn on left. Continue for about 500 feet follow signs to parking and entrance.

Stroller: Stroller accessible.

Bathrooms: Makeshift changing table in ladies & men's room.

Food: Vending machine nearby with snacks and drinks, OK to bring sippy cups, bottles, and toddler snacks. Picnic tables outside.

The Scoop:

Anchors away! Cheerfully decorated with fish nets, sea shells, and buoys, this small museum has plenty to offer for **children of all ages**. The tiniest tots will appreciate rooting around in a kid-sized boat filled with rice. Slightly older children can take advantage of the marble runs, pulleys, lego and other toy stations aimed at stimulating creativity and a sense of scientific discovery at the same time. The museum's location **in the heart of Port Jefferson** makes it a great stop on a day trip to this picturesque village (reviewed in Chapter 3), and just steps from the museum is a **lovely waterfront park** with paved paths.

Nature Centers

The Nature Centers reviewed in this section are small and won't take long to tour. So while they are not worth making a day trip for, locals living in the area may enjoy dropping by for a quick visit. Little ones will be treated to a close encounter with the natural world, and it's always fun to do something a little different.

If the weather is nice, an extended visit may be planned as all three places are surrounded by nature preserves with paved trails that are ideal for strollers.

Theodore Roosevelt Nature Center

Ocean Pkwy at "West End" of Jones Beach, Wantagh
Nassau, Town of Hempstead
516-679-7254, http://nysparks.state.ny.us

Activities: Marine exhibits about local ecosystem, nature programs for ages 3 and up. Boardwalk loop through sand dunes for quick outdoor stroll.

Age: Large yet contained space for toddlers to explore; crayons, babies can accompany older siblings who participate, and enjoy the adjacent play area.

Timing: Open weekends, year-round, 10-4pm.

Duration: An hour or less.

Fees: State park vehicle fee $8 during summer season; no charge other times of the year.

Finding It: Northern State Pkwy to Meadowbrook or Wantagh Pkwy; head south to end & follow signs to Jones Beach, then follow signs for Nature Center located on the "West End".

Parking: Good; large parking lot close to entrance.

Stroller: Nature center and boardwalk trail completely stroller-accessible.

Bathrooms: Diaper changing facilities in ladies room.

Food: None served but bagged lunch welcome at outdoor picnic tables.

The Scoop:

At the Theodore Roosevelt Nature Center, little ones can learn all about the ocean in the children's play area which features an assortment of **picture books, puzzles, and puppets**. It's manageable size makes it a good place to meet for a playdate, and it's easy to keep an eye on multiple children.

The **children's programs (ages 3-5)** are wonderful with a focus on hands-on activities exploring the natural world. Call for schedule or to get on the mailing list.

Tackapausha Museum

Washington Avenue, Seaford, Nassau
516-571-7443

Activities: Animal exhibits, animal shows some weekends.

Age: Toddlers and up.

Timing: Wed-Sat, 10-4pm, Sun, 1-4pm.

Duration: Less than an hour.

Fees: Adults, $3; children 5-12, $2; under 5, free.

Finding It: Take LIE to exit 44 south OR Southern State Pkwy to Rte 135/ Seaford-Oyster Bay Expwy; go south on Rte 135 & take Merrick Rd exit; head east on Merrick Rd about ½ mile & turn left onto Washington Ave; entrance on right.

Parking: Good; dedicated parking lot close to entrance.

Stroller: Not ideal; need to take stroller up a few steps to get into building, and downstairs for bathroom; nature preserve trail not too stroller-accessible.

Bathrooms: No diaper changing facilities in restrooms.

Food: None served, no dining facilities; OK to bring baby bottle and snacks.

The Scoop:

If you happen to be **in the neighborhood**, a quick jaunt to this small natural history museum can make for a pleasant diversion. The exhibits of local animals, plants, and geology are basic and a bit old, but the **dinosaur diorama** had my T-Rex-obsessed toddler enthralled as he tried to identify the different species on display. The **live bat exhibit** was pretty cool and you can call to find out when their animal show is and time your visit accordingly.

94

Center for Science, Teaching and Learning

1 Tanglewood Road, Rockville Centre, Nassau
516-764-0045, www.cstl.org

Activities: Small indoor reptile exhibit, nature trails, outdoor children's area with sandbox, puppets. Mommy and Me programs on occasion; call for details.

Age: Stroller-bound babies and up.

Timing: Open Wed-Sun, 10-4pm.

Duration: Half an hour tops indoors; longer if you choose to explore the preserve grounds.

Fees: $6/person; children under 1, free.

Finding It: Southern State: Exit 19S onto Peninsula Blvd. Make right onto Maine Ave. Follow to end.

Parking: A few parking spots by entrance, plentiful street parking nearby.

Stroller: Preserve & center are stroller-accessible.

Bathrooms: No diaper changing facilities in the restrooms.

Food: None served, OK to bring sippy cup or bottle; OK to bring food & eat at outdoor picnic tables.

The Scoop:

This **tiny indoor space** is only worth visiting if you live close by and the weather is decent enough to take a quick stroll of the preserve grounds (and feed the resident horse). Inside, the dozen or so viewing tanks offer toddlers a close-up glimpse of **snakes, lizards,** and parrots. Ask for the "exhibit guide", so they can make a game out of matching the pictures of the animals in the brochure with the living thing. In the small room, caregivers can sit on the bench and relax for a minute without having to worry about kids wandering away. But with those limited attention spans, it won't be long before they want to move on.

Open Play: Drop in Fun

From late November when the big chill hits, to early April when the first buds appear on the trees, **"open play"** sessions are my salvation. The facilities vary in size and features, but the basic concept is an **indoor, open space** designed for **little ones** to romp in.

Most of these places pay their bills by hosting birthday parties, and then set aside a few hours a week for **'open play'** when you can simply **drop in, pay the fee, and play**. Little ones, ranging from crawlers to their school-age siblings can take advantage of a generous collection of toys, climbing equipment, and other kid-friendly props which present a novel change from the toys at home.

While the places listed in this section are generally **clean, safe and well maintained**, accidents can happen, and it's up to the caregiver to be **vigilant** and keep a constant eye on the child.

Generally no food or drink allowed in play areas, but staff seems to look the other way at sippy cups, bottles and the occasional cheerios.

Visit Tip: Bring Socks
Make sure you have socks for both you and your child; they are required at most play spaces. You might even keep a spare pair in the car during flip flop season.

The Children's Safari

6 Rockaway Ave., Valley Stream, Nassau
Nassau, Town of Hempstead
516-872-2600
www.thechildrenssafari.com

Activities: Open play, classes for 10 months & up.

Age: Crawlers on up to about 7 years.

Timing: Usually Mon-Fri for open play. Call for hours.

Duration: 1-2 hours.

Fees: $11 per child all day for open play.

Finding It: Southern State to exit 15S, head South on Corona Ave, bear left (name changes to Rockaway) and go ~1 mile to light intersection with Merritt Rd. Look for it on the right.

Parking: Not ideal - street parking or make 1st right past building and park in Municipal parking lot (9).

Stroller: Completely stroller-accessible.

Bathrooms: Diaper changing station in the restroom.

Food: Snack bar on-site with dining area. No outside food allowed, bottles/sippy cups OK to consume in designated dining area.

The Scoop:

This safari has **no live animals** but it does have four distinct options for play; a toy area with everything from doll houses to train sets, a climbing structure with tunnels and slides, a **sandbox** filled with real sand, a special section with soft, interactive objects especially for crawlers.

Active Kidz

210 Forest Dr. East Hills, Nassau
516-621-6600
www.activekidzlongisland.com

Activities: Open play, sports & yoga classes for ages 1-8.

Age: Crawlers on up.

Timing: Open daily, call for open play schedule.

Duration: 1-2 hours.

Fees: $4, 10/child all depending on play space used.

Finding It: LIE (495) west to exit 39N, right at light onto Glen Cove Rd, left onto Northern Blvd. At 2nd light make left onto Forest Dr. Follow signs all the way to the end.

Parking: Plentiful in dedicated parking lot.

Stroller: Completely stroller-accessible.

Bathrooms: Diaper-changing table in ladies & men's rooms.

Food: Snack bar with dining area serves drinks and chips/pretzels. OK to bring your own food and eat in the dining area. Water provided by staff.

The Scoop:

The **giant, multi-level climbing, sliding structure** is the main attraction for the open play sessions which tend to draw a toddling crowd. Kids seem to love ascending this obstacle course of ropes and tunnels where they can wave to mama from way up on high. For crawlers there is a **separate "toddler room"**, a mellower alternative containing gym mats, soft climbing equipment, and picture books. Children over four years might try out the **rock climbing wall** for an additional fee.

Doodle Bugs Gym

145 Voice Road, Carle Place, Nassau
Nassau, Town of North Hempstead
516-747-9120

Activities: Open play, baby/toddler classes.

Age: Crawlers on up.

Timing: Weekdays & Saturdays. Call for schedule.

Duration: 1- 1 ½ hours.

Fees: Non-members, $8; free for kids enrolled in class.

Finding It: LIE to exit 39 south (Glen Cove Rd); go south on Glen Cove Rd; turn right onto Voice Rd. (light intersection with lots of stores); at first corner make right into L-shaped shopping strip. Entrance on left.

Parking: Strip mall parking with spots just outside gym.

Stroller: Completely stroller-accessible.

Bathrooms: No diaper-changing area, but the gym floor works fine in a pinch.

Food: None served; OK to bring your own food, little tables to eat at; pizza place a few stores down.

The Scoop:

Your child can't go very far in this **compact gym**, and parents **who are tired of chasing toddlers** can sit back and watch for a change. But the smallish space does pack in lots of fun soft play equipment; vinyl blocks to climb over, a mini trampoline, as well as tunnels and slides that are suitable for late stage crawling babies.

Once Upon a Treetop

151 Dupont St. Plainview, Nassau
516-349-1140
www.onceuponatreetop.com

Activities: Open play in a **wonderful play "town."**

Classes: Many offerings for newborns on up in music, art, theater, computer, pre-reading, and yoga.

Age: Toddlers to about 7 years.

Timing: Weekdays & some Saturdays. Call for hours.

Duration: 1-3 hours.

Fees: $12 for walkers; $6 for crawlers; infants free.

Finding It: LIE (495) to exit 46 (Sunnyside Blvd).
From east: turn right onto Sunnyside Blvd.
From west: turn left onto Sunnyside Blvd.
From Sunnyside Blvd. turn right onto Fairchild, left at Dupont St. Building will be on right.

Parking: Parking lot right outside building.

Stroller: Completely stroller-accessible, strollers not allowed in "town" play area to keep floor clean for crawlers, so there is a stroller parking area.

Bathrooms: Changing table in men's & women's restrooms.

Food: Outside food & drink welcome for consumption in the "mess hall" dining area only. Delivery menus available from local restaurants.

The Scoop:

Take a walk down "Main Street" and let your child explore this **mini town** outfitted with a **diner, school, puppet theater,** and train depot. Well designed with quaint touches such as street lamps. "Once Upon a Treetop" is truly a novel experience and **worth a trip even from far away.**

Little Sunshine Playcenter

299 Raft Avenue, Sayville, Town of Islip, Suffolk
631-563-PLAY
www.littlesunshineplaycenter.com

Activities: Open play, classes for babies to 4 years.

Age: Crawlers on up; tons of toys, access to arts & crafts supplies.

Duration: 1-2 hours.

Fees: Adults, free; $5 per child, free trial class offered.

Finding It: Located off the service road on south side of Sunrise Hwy between exits 50 & 51; website has detailed directions.

Parking: Large lot with plenty of parking near entrance.

Stroller: Easy; just wheel your stroller right in.

Bathrooms: Diaper changing table.

The Scoop:

This bright, **open space** features a **treasure trove of toys** including a **play kitchen, doll house, train set**, and parking garage filled with cars. Slightly older toddlers can help themselves to bins full of **arts and crafts supplies,** and it's a great opportunity for your aspiring sculptor to create a playdoh **masterpiece** without messing up your own house.

Wood Kingdom

111 Milbar Blvd, **Farmingdale**, Nassau, 631-845-3804
544 Middle Country Rd, **Coram**, Suffolk, 631- 698-0212
www.woodkingdom.com

Activities: Open play in indoor playground.

Age: Toddlers & up.

Timing: Call for open play schedule; better when there isn't a birthday party going on so ask.

Duration: 1½ hours.

Fees: Adults, free; children, $5.

Finding It: *Coram* location: on Middle Country Rd between Rte 83 & Rte 112.
Farmingdale location: Milbar Blvd, 1 block east of Rte 110, just south of Adventureland.

Parking: Lot right at the entrance.

Stroller: Easy; stroll right in and leave it wherever.

Bathrooms: Diaper changing stations near restrooms.

Food: Snack, juice, & coffee included in price; OK to bring your own snack and eat at their tables.

The Scoop:

Although it's basically a big **store** that sells swing sets for your backyard, Wood Kingdom's "open play" time offers a fun escape for the energetic toddler on a cold winter day. Their **indoor playground** has several play sets with slides, ladders, and climbing equipment. Just keep an eye on little ones when older children are present; it can get a touch rough! That said, it's an easy place to take siblings since it's fun for kids of varying ages.

Orly's Treehouse

1000 Shames Drive, Westbury, Town of N. Hempstead, Nassau
516-333-2277
www.orlystreehouse.com

Activities: Open play in indoor playground, classes, monthly children's parties.

Age: Newborn to 7 for classes, open play for toddlers to about ~5 years.

Timing: Open daily, 9am-5pm.

Fees: $15 per child.

Finding It: Northern State Pkwy to Exit 34; turn right at light onto Brush Hollow Rd. Go ~1/3 mile & turn right onto Shames Dr. Entrance on left at 1000 Shames Dr.

Parking: Lot right at the entrance.

Stroller: Easy; stroll right in and leave it wherever.

Bathrooms: Diaper changing stations, nursing room.

Food: On-site café serves meals for adults and kids.

The Scoop:

This colorful, artfully designed, **one-stop recreation center** for new families features a café, a wide selection of classes, **an adult workout room**, and even a day spa (also for grownups.). The centerpiece of the play space is the tree house which is surrounded by themed sections including a pretend grocery store, an auto repair shop, and costumes for dress up. Drop in for open play or for a more festive introduction to the facility, check their website for the next monthly "party".

Let's Bounce

Party rooms featuring giant "inflatables" with slides, obstacle course, and other moon bounce equipment seem to be popping up all over the island recently. When not hosting a party, some of these places offer "**open play**" and M**ommy and Me classes** where toddlers can have a blast, thoroughly exhaust themselves, and sleep well for their parents at night.

Bouncers beware!
Don't go down head first

In addition to the rigorous workout, there is the added advantage that all that bouncing, climbing, and balancing gives them a "jumpstart" on their motor skill development. In fact, my kids don't come looking for me until their little foreheads are drenched with sweat, that is, unless they get a boo boo first.

Parental Patrol Advised

Those pliant surfaces look soft, but accidents do happen, and my sons have collided into each other, um, well, more often than I'd like to admit. My younger son even managed to fall over the side of one of these inflated walls, landing with a thud onto an unforgiving hard floor. The tears flowed for a few minutes, but with all those kids jumping for joy around him, it wasn't long before he was bouncing again. I guess that's why they make you sign a waiver exempting them from liability before your little ones get to go on.

Generally however, under the watch of a vigilant caregiver, these places offer a clean, colorful, and contained area for children to romp when the local playground isn't an option. Here are some thoughts to keep in mind when planning your visit.

Guidelines for Optimal Bouncing

- *Timing* – some places charge by the hour, others for the entire session. I found that an hour is plenty long enough for them to get a good workout.

- *Bring socks!* They are required at all places. Some have them for sale for forgetful parents.

- *Eat beforehand* – outside food is not permitted in the bouncy rooms, though some places have a lobby-type area to feed toddler a quick snack.

- *Bring water* – in bottles or sippy cups. They get thirsty.

- *Strollers welcome* – all the places reviewed are stroller accessible and have plenty of space to accommodate strollers.

- *Attendants* – some of these places have attendants during open play which adds a measure of safety; others don't.

- *Keeping it mellow* – time your trip for when the bigger kids are in school and it's less busy.

- *Open play hours don't work for your schedule?* Gather a few parents and set up your playgroup time at your convenience (about 5-10 kid minimum).

- *Avoiding cooties* – exposure to germs are unavoidable but most of these places have sani-soap dispensers right in the bouncing room for easy access.

Let's Bounce 'N' Party

602 N. Wellwood Ave, Lindenhurst, Suffolk
631-226-8623, www.letsbouncenparty.com

Activities: Open play in large room with ~4 inflatables, Mommy & Me classes.

Age: Toddlers on up for open play.

Timing: Many open play during week and weekends. Call or check website for latest schedule.

Fees: Open play - $10 for 1st kid, ½ price 2nd kid.

Finding It: *From East:* Take Southern State Pkwy West to exit 35 (Lindenhurst). Merge onto County Rte 3/N Wellwood Ave. It's on left in Sunrise Plaza shopping center (next to Outback Steakhouse). *From West:* Take Southern State Pkwy West to exit 33. (Rte 109 East/Babylon). Merge onto Farmingdale Rd/Rte 109. Turn right onto Rte 3 (Wellwood Ave). It's on left in Sunrise Plaza shopping center (next to Outback Steakhouse).

Parking: Lot right at the entrance.

Food: No outside food allowed; sippy cups, bottles OK. Pizza & bagel shop across the parking lot.

Bathrooms: Diaper changing stations in the bathroom.

The Scoop:

Started by three moms, this **low-key, friendly place** is operated with the needs of toddlers in mind; the bathroom has a kid-size toilet, step stool to reach the sink, and even a potty. There is also a lobby area with air hockey and a mini bowling game, as well as a separate room for Mommy and Me classes.

Jump

151 Dominion Blvd. Ronkonkoma, Suffolk
631-585-JUMP
www.jumparties.com

Activities: Open play in two rooms of huge inflatables, game room with coin operated toddler rides.

Age: Ages 3 & up.

Timing: Call or check website for open play.

Fees: $14-$16 per child for open play; no fee for adults and children under three.

Finding It: LIE (495) to exit 59. Take Ocean Ave (CR 93) south. After ~3/4 mile bear left at fork onto Lakeland Ave. Go ~1/2 mile and turn right onto Union Pkwy. Turn left onto Dominion Blvd.

Bathrooms: No diaper changing stations, ample space around to improvise.

Food: No outside food allowed, sippy cups, bottles OK. Pizza available to order.

The Scoop:

At the open play sessions, Jump has **"counselors"** on hand to watch the kids so parents can relax somewhat. The two spacious rooms have terrific, colorful bouncy courses including a **"ball blaster"**. The adjacent game room is a big draw for small children, and one of the open play packages includes coins to operate the toddler rides. On the other hand, it's a hindrance if you're only interested in the inflatables since they will likely be nagging you to visit the **game room** too.

The management welcomes children with autism and other challenges, and can provide extra counselors to meet their needs.

Kangaroo Kids

1015 Grand Blvd. Deer Park, Suffolk
631-871-8762, www.kangarookidsparty.com

Activities:	Open play on inflatables, playgroups by appointment.
Age:	Toddlers to about 8 years.
Timing:	Call for open play schedule.
Fees:	$10 for the first child; sibling discounts.
Finding It:	Ok, I admit to being directionally-challenged, but this place was hard to find. Print off the detailed directions on their website and keep in mind that there are **two Industry Streets** and you should take EAST Industry, the **2nd one**. Also park at the Saf-t-Swim parking lot and walk into the Saf-T-Swim building entrance. You'll find it there.
Bathrooms:	Changing station in restroom down the hall.
Food:	Sippy cup/bottle OK, no outside food allowed. Vending machines in lobby, water cooler. Tanger Outlets-www.tangeroutlet.com/deerpark.

The Scoop:

With three inflatables, Kangaroo Kids is smaller than most of the places out there, but the **contained space** has the advantage of making it easier to keep an eye on little ones without having to chase them around. Here, parents tend to settle down into a chair and chat while their children explore. I also felt that the fact that the **bounce house**, slides and inflatable obstacle course were on a smaller scale made them more approachable for toddlers. There are also some toys of interest to crawling siblings, as well as an air hockey table for school age kids.

For some, a trip to Kangaroo Kids may be a bit out of the way, but keep in mind that **Tanger Outlets** at the Arches, a shoppers paradise, is right there.

Bouncers & Slydos

1835 New Highway, Farmingdale, Nassau
631-752-2324
www.bouncersandslydos.com

Activities: Open play in giant room with 10+ inflatables.

Age: Toddlers on up.

Timing: Call or check website for open play.

Fees: $12 per child for open play.

Finding It: *From LIE:* take exit 49S, make right turn onto Rte 110. Go ~2 miles & turn left onto Ruland Rd (Costco on corner). At 1st light make right onto Republic which turns into New Highway. Building is ~1 mile on left.

Bathrooms: Diaper changing station in restrooms.

Food: No outside food allowed, sippy cups/bottles OK.

The Scoop:

Housed in a **gigantic** warehouse space, Bouncers & Slydos has lots of inflatable diversions varying in sizes, activities and themes. During **Toddler Time**, a popular open-play session, the inflatable courses suitable for small children are blown up. There your toddler might find the "soccer field" where he or she can practice kicking a soft ball into an inflatable goal.

Pump It Up

135 Dupont St., Plainview, 516-575-2300
1750 Arctic Ave., Bohemia, 631-563-3100
250 Community Drive, Great Neck, 516-466-7867
www.pumpitupparty.com

Activities: Open play in two large rooms of inflatables. Classes offered at select locations.

Age: Ages 2 and up.

Timing: Call for open play schedule.

Fees: About $11-$14 per child depending on site.

Finding It: Check website for directions.

Bathrooms: Diaper changing stations in restrooms.

Food: No outside food allowed. Bottles/sippy cups OK.

The Scoop:

Primarily devoted to **birthday parties**, Pump It Up offers open play at certain times and locations. If you live close to one, give them a buzz; its nice to know that you have an indoor playground nearby on a dreary day. At Pump It Up, the inflatables are somewhat determined by height, which is a good way to separate the tough older kids from the precious, little ones. For example, there is usually a bounce house just for children 34" and smaller where a **crawler can go for a roll** and tumble without worrying about getting bowled over by a big kid.

Mommy and Me classes are held at some locations, for children as young as 18 months old. A sampling of classes that have been offered in the past include "Terrific Tots", "Jump Start Your ABCs", and "Music Go Round".

Fun 4 All

200 Wilson St., Port Jefferson Station, Suffolk
631-331-9000

Activities: Inflatable slides and obstacle courses.

Age: Toddlers on up; little ones tend to gravitate to some of the play equipment intended for bigger kids requiring close adult supervision.

Timing: Daily 10-8pm, weekends can get crowded.

Duration: 1-2 hours.

Fees: Adults, free; children 2-15, $8.99; 1 year olds, $4.99.

Finding It: LIE to exit 64; follow Rte 112 (Port Jefferson and Patchogue Rd) north for about 8½ miles. Turn left onto Wilson St right before railroad tracks and you'll see entrance.

Parking: Excellent, park in their lot and stroll right In.

Stroller: Great; stroll right into the building and leave it wherever you please.

Bathrooms: Changing table in ladies room.

Food: Snack bar serving pizza, popcorn & soft drinks.

The Scoop:

With a selection of inflatable obstacle courses just for little ones, Fun 4 All is a good place to drop in and play on a rainy day. The **moon room** is also an interesting place to check out, though very small children might be tempted to eat the rubber "woodchips" that cover the floor.

The overall space is huge, and it can be challenging to **keep track of a wandering toddler**, particularly on weekends when it can get crowded, if not chaotic. As an extra safety measure though, **security bracelets** are issued.

Now Showing...

It's a few years off still until you can take baby to Broadway, but in the meantime here are some "shows" that can accommodate short attention spans and the occasional outburst. **Puppet performances** in particular are a wonderful way to introduce children to the world of theater. Long Island's many **model train hobbyists** also put on a show of sorts that always seems to delight toddlers.

Goat on a Boat Puppet Theater

Route 114 & East Union Street, Sag Harbor
Suffolk, Town of Southampton
631-725-4193, www.goatonaboat.org

Activities: Puppet shows and playgroups.

Age: Crawlers on up; good for toddler/ infant combo.

Parking: Street parking in front of the theater.

Timing: Programs & shows held weekday & weekend mornings; call or log on for latest schedule.

Duration: About an hour.

Fees: Puppet shows $8 for adults and big kids, $4 for children under 3 years; play groups are $20 for a single session, discounts for multiple classes and siblings.

Stroller: A few steps down to theater entrance where there's a place to park strollers.

Bathrooms: Mat provided in a separate room for changing baby's diaper; bathrooms in back.

Food: None served; sippy cups & kiddy snacks OK.

The Scoop:

The true star of this one-woman show is **Liz Joyce**. As the voice and hands behind the puppets that entertain children, she also manages to make the **grown-ups chuckle** with her witty puns and adult-oriented wisecracks. And though you won't get to see much of her face at the puppet shows, the **playgroups** are a whole different story. During these highly interactive sessions, this master "puppeteeress" is right there with all the babies and toddlers, **strumming on her banjo** and belting out favorite children's tunes that get everyone clapping hands and tapping toes.

The theater itself is located in a parish house behind a church and unlike traditional theaters, there are **no seats** to speak of; just grab a patch of the carpeted floor, and make yourself comfortable. This type of spectator format is especially **conducive to toddlers** afflicted with wanderlust - if they get restless, they can simply move around.

Some even get so taken in with the **"talking animals"** that they approach the stage, so don't be surprised if yours attempts to have a conversation with the puppets in the middle of the show.

Finding It:

LIE east to exit 70 (Manorville), head south on Rte 111 for several miles following signs for Rte 27 (Sunrise Hwy). When Rte 111 ends, road veers left and turns into Rte 27. Go east on Rte 27 for about 23 miles. Go through Village of Bridgehampton and take left at traffic light onto Sag Harbor Turnpike (Rte 79). Continue on Rte 79 about 4 miles until road changes name to Main St. Look for Whaling Museum at 200 Main St (it's a big white Greek Revival House with tall columns). Turn right at that corner onto Union St. Go a few blocks. At intersection with Rte 114 & Division St, you'll see Christ Episcopal Church across the street. Theater is in the building next door on East Union St.

Long Island
Puppet Theater & Museum

10 Heitz Place, Hicksville
Nassau, Town of Oyster Bay
516-932-5469
www.lipuppet.com

Activities: Puppet show.

Age: 18 months & up; good place to bring the infant/toddler sibling combo; occasionally young children may get frightened.

Finding It: Exit 11 off LIE; go south on Rte 107 past 4 traffic lights, make left just before the Sears onto Nevada St. At first light, make right onto Bay Ave. Follow to the end, and make right onto Heitz Pl. Theater is colorful building on right.

Timing: Frequent shows but hours vary, call or log on for show times.

Duration: About 1-1 ½ hours; actual puppet show lasts around 45 minutes.

Fees: Adults & Children, $10; under 1 year, free.

Parking: Very good; adjacent dedicated lot; arrive 15 minutes early for a spot closest to the entrance.

Stroller: Strollers are OK to bring if you think you'll need it, but the management prefers not to have too many strollers, as the space fills quickly.

Bathrooms: Good; bathroom has diaper changing table.

Food: No food or beverages served or permitted, unless you attend a "pizza show."

The Scoop:

The fairy tale begins as you approach this **funky little theater** painted in bright, whimsical colors. We were a little early the day we visited, and the front door was actually locked, causing me to wonder if I had gotten the show times mixed up. But sure enough, a lady responded to my knocking, and ushered us inside.

But **arriving 15-20 minutes** or so before the show allows ample time to check out the small collection of hand-crafted, **international puppets on display**. There is also a miniature, **toddler-scale theater** with a number of hand puppets for children to experiment with.

Grandparents take note! This is a relatively easy place to take grandchildren since they can't get very far in the small, enclosed space. One couple I spoke to were bringing their granddaughter for the third time and noted that the novelty hadn't worn off because the shows change frequently.

We happened to see the **"Little Mermaid"** which was performed by several colorful and elaborately-decorated puppets on a glittering stage. The children in the audience ranged in age from a **6 month old baby** to her **ten year old brother**, and everyone seemed duly entertained. Well, that is, everyone except my 18-month son who suddenly got spooked by the witch puppet. So we stepped back into the lobby for a short break, and returned to enjoy the rest of the performance.

It's definitely a cute, unusual place to visit, and afterwards you can drop by the small **Hicksville Gregory Museum** across the street, which focuses on Earth Science (516-822-7505).

Model Train Shows

Tickets please! If your toddler is a train enthusiast, he or she will enjoy visiting an open house held by one of the handful of **model railroad clubs** across the island. Run by grown-up train hobbyists who build layouts for everything from **steam engines** to **diesel locomotives**, these clubs periodically put on shows for the public.

Since these clubs operate on tight budgets, don't expect sparkling facilities. Held in non-profit venues such as **churches, community centers,** and VFW buildings, often for fundraising purposes, the shows are really a labor of love put on by **volunteers** who bring their own trains and tracks, and then toil away for hours to set it all up for visitors.

My son Ben had just turned two when we took him to a layout featuring N-scale trains held at a church in East Northport. We got there about half an hour into the show only to discover the members were still setting up the tracks, and some of the modules hadn't arrived yet. But such technical difficulties are par for the course, and soon enough a Conrail engine was up and running, **pulling more than a dozen freight cars** over bridges, past farm lands, and through quaint miniature towns replete with working traffic lights.

Well the effect on the children present was nothing short of magical. Even the **tinier tots** seemed to be completely entranced by the sights and sounds of the trains chugging along the tracks, and I was amazed at how long their **attention span** lasted. Unfortunately for their parents and **grandparents** however, the only way for small children to get a close-up look was to physically lift them, and after awhile I thought my back was going to buckle under the weight of my forty pounder.

I'm not sure whether it's the work of nature or nurture, but most of the aspiring train conductors I know are boys. I have met quite a few **female train enthusiasts** though, and hope that gender bias won't preclude their parents from taking part in this type of activity.

The only drawback to these events is you have to keep a lookout for when they happen. Usually the **open house dates** are set months in advance and are posted on the **clubs' websites**, that is, if they have one. But to see your aspiring little conductor mesmerized by the choo choos is probably worth the trouble of marking the day on your calendar. Some of the more notable model train clubs and layouts are listed below.

Central Operating Lines Model Railroad Club
Ronkonkoma, 631-472-3395, 631-661-9345
www.trainweb.org/centoplines/
Website lists upcoming open house dates,
typically in Fall & Winter.

West Island Model Railroad Club
485 South Broadway, Hicksville
516-433-6600
www.trainweb.org/westisland/
Website lists upcoming open house dates.

Wrong Island Railroad
This is a store with a train layout.
www.wrongislandrailroad.com
Lake Ronkonkoma, 631-467-1222
Layout usually operates weekends
in December and January.

Rockville Centre Model Railroaders
Rockville Centre, 516-594-1654
www.rvcmr.org
Check website for next open house.

Libraries – A Toy Story

Shhhh...people are trying to read! With its rooms lined with bookshelves and sounds limited to the occasional cough or shuffling foot steps, the library hardly seems an appropriate place to bring a boisterous baby.

Well the silent library has become a thing of the past. In recent years, many have dramatically expanded and upgraded their service offerings for youngsters. Usually, it's simply a matter of getting the stroller past the main reading room and into the **children's section** which is sequestered off in a fairly soundproof zone. And since most libraries are wheelchair, and therefore **stroller-accessible**, you can cruise right in without having to bother collapsing the stroller. Moreover, the librarians are accustomed to frequent cheerful, (or tearful) outbursts, and glad to see new faces at this **free,** but all too often **underutilized resource**.

It's not just books either; many libraries carry **toys, blocks, puzzles** and other diversions for the under three set, presenting a fresh alternative to the tired, well-worn toys at home.

Because **all libraries are open to the public**, you don't have to share their zip code to gain access. In fact, I still **rotate** between a few different libraries to get a change of scene for both me and my boys. They just ask that you clean up after yourselves when you finish.

As for interactive programs like **baby/toddler classes**, it's hard to beat the offerings at a good library. Many libraries feature programs that welcome **infants**, and it's an economical way to learn mother goose rhymes while meeting other new parents in the neighborhood.

> ### Information on Libraries in
>
> **Suffolk:** www.suffolk.lib.ny.us
> 631-286-1600
>
> **Nassau**: www.nassaulibrary.org
> 516-292-8920

One of my favorite library events is **evening "story time."** These popular programs tend to fill up fast but the sight of all those **pajama-clad babies** and toddlers is just too cute to pass up! I took Ben when he was two and his brother Tycho was just four months. Admittedly, it was a bit challenging to get them both fed, bathed, and into the library on time for the 7pm start. But we made it, and I hoped that the soothing sounds of a librarian reading books would help wind Ben down for the night.

Well I couldn't have been more wrong! The sight of all those children was just too exciting and he stayed in my lap for about eight seconds before leaping up to make his rounds. Of course most of the other toddlers sat placidly in their parent's lap listening to the story, and I couldn't understand why my son chose to be the Tasmanian devil that evening. But naturally there are times when Ben does cooperate, and it was one of the easier places to take him when I had a newborn.

If you aren't on the **mailing list** for your local library already, you may want to start by getting on it. That way you can get a heads up on **upcoming programs**. The majority of Long Island's libraries post their events calendar on their website, and you may just find out about a **free puppet show** or **musical performance** that will delight toddler!

Book Stores – Tales for Tots

Even before I had children, **book stores** were a favorite rainy day haunt. I recently read though, that only one in seven Americans visits book stores, and it's a real pity. But regardless of whether you were a book store patron *before* you had a baby, **now is *the* time** to discover this wonderful baby friendly oasis.

With their extensive children sections and story time programs, book stores embrace new parents, **grandparents, nannies,** and other caregivers of little ones. And **noise?** Sure! Babies cry and toddlers pull books off the shelves, but in general, the mayhem I had expected never really materialized. Instead there were cute **picture books** to 'read' with baby, not to mention "grown-up" books to peruse when baby nodded off in the stroller. To top it all, **it's free,** although I tend to do a lot of damage on my credit card in these places. But I justify my purchases by reminding myself that books are part of the education process.

I was also never attuned to how "baby friendly" book stores could be until I attempted to bring mine into one. **Parking** is usually convenient and even the smaller stores can be very **stroller-accessible** with large entrances and ample space between the aisles for a four wheeler. Many have **diaper changing stations** in the ladies room, and the Barnes and Noble in Manhasset even has one in the men's room! (So there's absolutely no excuse for dad not to go spend quality time with toddler while mom relaxes at home). And if the child or daddy gets the munchies while there, they can head over to the **café** which most book stores now have right on the premises.

I find that guys often like to have something concrete to do with children, and the **free "story-time"** held at many book stores provides a **fun, defined activity** to do together. At these events, the little ones gather around a "bookstorian" who reads them a brightly illustrated picture book.

Generally there is no age limit for these events and I have seen babies as young as **three months** snuggled up to mommy's chest in a frontal carrier.

Toddlers tend to roam and fidget so if your little one sits contentedly for the entire reading, it's the exception. I found that my son's ability to sit still depended on a host of factors including when he last ate, napped, pooped or God knows what else. But when the weather was lousy, and I had both a toddler and infant to entertain, bookstores served as a nice refuge (although it's easy to lose sight of the older one amidst the aisles of books).

One of the best aspects of book stores is they're open during most of baby's waking hours **including evenings and weekends** when other indoor venues are more likely to be closed. While the midnight trip with an insomniac baby is not very likely, it's nice to know you can pop in almost any time without having to plan ahead and reserve a spot like you do with the classes.

Listed below are some book stores on Long Island. The Barnes and Noble and Borders chains are generally a safe bet for those seeking baby-friendly facilities. But it's worth checking out the independent book sellers as well; many have wonderful children's sections and welcome even the youngest of "readers."

BookHampton   www.bookhampton.com

East Hampton
20 Main St
631-324-4939

Southampton
91 Main St
631-283-0270

Sag Harbor
20 Main St
631-725-8425

Amagansett Square
154 Main St. Amagansett
631-267-5405

Barnes & Noble   www.barnesandnoble.com

Bay Shore
842 Sunrise Hwy
631-206-0198

Commack
5001 Jericho Tpke
631-462-0896

New Hyde Park
1424 Union Tpke
516-437-0324

Carle Place
91 Old Country Rd
516-741-9850

Massapequa
5224 Sunrise Hwy
516-541-1456

Manhasset
1542 Northern Blvd
516-365-6723

Huntington Station
380 Walt Whitman Rd
631-421-9886

Lake Grove
600 Smith Haven Mall
631-724-0341

East Northport
4000 E. Jerciho Tpke
631-462-0208

Borders Books   www.borders.com

Farmingdale
231 Airport Blvd.
631-752-0194

Syosset
425 Jericho Tpke
516-496-3934

Westbury
1260 Old Country Rd
516-683-8700

Bohemia
5151 Sunrise Hwy
631-244-7496

Riverhead
1500 Old Country Rd
631-284-2222

Commack
68 Vets Mem. Hwy
631-462-0569

Stony Brook
2130 Nesconsett Hwy
631-979-0500

Massapequa
460 Sunrise Mall
516-795-3683

Book Revue
www.bookrevue.com
313 New York Ave
Huntington Village
631-271-1442

The Open Book
In Town of Southampton
128A Main St
Westhampton Beach
631-288-2120

5

New Parents, New Friendships

Can We Talk?

Interested in **meeting fellow new parents** and their kids? In this chapter you'll find several venues for bringing moms (and dads) together. Ranging from **luncheons** at nice restaurants, to **discussion groups**, to organized **play dates** at parks, these "meet" markets draw all kinds of fun, interesting women. It's quite a cross-section of people too; I've met high powered professionals on break from Corporate America, journalists, teachers, and even a professional clown!

Regardless, it's NOT an intimidating environment and if your baby tends to cry at inopportune moments, you're sure to find a **sympathetic audience** here. Not sure about it? Many groups hold open houses, where you're welcome to come and check it out with no obligation to join.

National Association
Of Mothers' Centers

Throughout Long Island
877.939.MOMS
www.motherscenters.org

The National Association of Mother's Centers **(NAMC)** is a wonderful organization that welcomes moms (and dads) to share the joys and challenges of parenting, and life in general.

Each Mother Center offers **discussion groups**, which strive to provide a **supportive** and **non-judgmental** forum for exchanging ideas and opinions. The discussion group topics run the gamut; here's a sample of the types of themes discussed at a typical center:

- ▶ The Trials & Triumphs of Moms and their Toddlers
- ▶ Women and Friendships
- ▶ Effective Parenting
- ▶ Children's Eating Habits and Nutrition
- ▶ Beginnings of Motherhood

 Depending on the activity, the baby can remain by mommy's side or play in an adjoining room under the supervision of a caregiver. **Childcare** fees are quite reasonable and if an episode of **separation anxiety** strikes, mom only has to walk a few steps to soothe him or her.

Although best known for their discussion groups, Mother Centers offer other social activities as well such as **Couple's Night Out, Mommy & Me, Babysitting Co-ops, Gardening Groups, and Book Clubs.**

```
Annual Membership: $30-$60 depending on center
```

A good, non-committal way to get more acquainted with a mother center is to attend an **open house**. Typically held in September and January, the open houses offer a free and informal orientation for all moms and their little ones.

NAMC Locations In Nassau:

West Hempstead (called Unity Circle)
516-486-2047

Wantagh
516-679-4641
www.Midshoremotherscenter.org

East Rockaway
516-599-7788
www.swnassauny.motherscenter.org

Offered through public libraries, ask for Mother's group

Baldwin	Long Beach	Port Washington
516-223-6228	516-432-7201	516-883-4400

NAMC Locations In Suffolk:

Northport
631 834 7192
www.northportmotherscenter.org

Sayville
631-680-9106
www.motherscenterofthesouthshore.com

Setauket
631-689-2827
www.suffolkmotherscenter.com

Huntington
631-271-3811
www.huntington.americantowns.com
(click on orgs, VPC)

Offered through public libraries, ask for Mother's group

Bellport	Centereach
631-286-0818	631-585-9393, ext 143

Huntington Station
631-549-4411
www.bigtent.com/groups/shmc

Note: If there's no Mother Center in your immediate area, consider **starting one yourself!** The National office is glad to provide resources and support to assist moms with launching a new center in their community.

M.O.M.S. Club

Brookhaven/Islip/Smithtown, Babylon, Suffolk County
www.momsclub.org, click on 'Chapter Links'
Most chapters have a website with specific contact info

With chapters in almost all fifty states, the International MOMS Club has brought thousands of new mothers together over the **twenty plus years** it's been in operation. Currently the Long Island chapters of the MOMS Club, which stands for **Moms Offering Moms Support**, are active in the Brookhaven and Islip area.

Completely run by volunteer moms, the club certainly provides **support to new mothers**, but it also offers a lively social calendar with events such as **Moms' Night Out, information seminars,** and **book clubs**.

Have baby, will travel...

One of the most popular activities, however, is the **organized playgroup**. As a new mother, I found myself not only seeking out the companionship of fellow moms, but also gravitating toward those with children close to the ages of mine. The MOMS club meets this need by offering **age-specific** play groups. In foul weather the groups convene at **members' homes** or at indoor **"play spaces."** In warm weather, they make **field trips** to fun places like local **zoos, parks, and beaches**. If you **recently moved to the area**, it's a great way to find out about some baby-friendly places nearby.

Trying It: Attend a monthly meeting. No fee.

Cost: Annual membership is $20- $25.

La Leche League

Throughout Long Island
800-lal-eche
847-519-7730 for breastfeeding counselor in area
www.lalecheleague.org

La Leche League is an international **nonprofit** organization that seeks to provide support and information about breastfeeding. Over fifteen groups convene around the island and anyone **breastfeeding (or pregnant)** is welcome to attend one of their monthly meetings to check it out.

For some reason, prior to attending a meeting, I had the impression that La Leche League was a group of hard core breastfeeding fanatics that would scorn me for supplementing my baby's diet of breast milk with formula. I honestly don't know why I thought this but I was pleasantly surprised to discover a fairly nonjudgmental atmosphere and even a few other moms whose children were bottle fed with formula. The group leaders are schooled in the **La Leche philosophy** though, and encourage mothers to breastfeed their babies as long as possible. In fact, the leader of one of the groups I attended had nursed her children until they were three years old!

Checking it out

The annual membership fee is about $40, but it's **free to attend a monthly meeting** and there is no obligation to join. To obtain information on active groups, call their 800 number and leave your address on their voicemail. Someone will mail you information about La Leche meetings in your area. With over a dozen active groups running on Long Island the last time I looked, you will likely find a meeting fairly close to home. You can also go to their website for a list of current **local leaders** and their phone numbers.

Mingling Moms

Westbury
917-733-7705
www.minglingmoms.com
About $165 for four lunches

Remember going out for a bite with a girlfriend, way back when before baby arrived? Do you find yourself pining for those days when you could enjoy a meal without every other diner shooting you and your extremely unpredictable baby exasperated looks? Well then consider Mingling Moms. At their lunch gatherings, new moms get to go to a **nice restaurant**, eat a **three course, gourmet meal**, and shoot the breeze with the gals, all in the company of their babies.

"Whining" and Dining

Since the luncheons are designed especially for mothers of **babies under 12 months**, the place is brimming with strollers, and there are convenient provisions for changing diapers and **warming bottles**. It's an ideal testing ground for moms that are nervous about **taking an infant out in public**, and as Erica Logiudice, the founder likes to say, "It's the 1st stop on the train ride through mommyhood." Babies get their entertainment needs met as well with **"circle-time"** when the mommies sing songs and do finger-plays with baby on their lap.

Fostering friendships that extend beyond the luncheons is strongly encouraged and table seating is arranged according to town of residence. I sat next to a fellow Huntington resident for example, and it wasn't long before we found out we had **a lot in common** including a stint of urban living in Manhattan.

128

Center for Parents and Children

12 Main Avenue, Sea Cliff
(Between Sea Cliff Ave. & Glen Ave.) good directions on website
516-671-4141
www.centerforparentsandchildren.org

New parents living anywhere in the vicinity of the North Shore town of **Glen Cove** owe it to themselves to drop by the Center for Parents and Children.

Home, Sweet Home

Occupying the space of an actual home, the center provides a **comfortable and inviting setting** for parents and children to gather. What was once the house's formal dining room has been converted into a **children's play area.** The adjacent family room, which lets the sun shine in through its many windows, has been set up for **adult discussion groups**. And since there's no door separating the two rooms, the little ones are able to play with mom visible, which helps stave off the occasional bout of **separation anxiety**.

The Center also offers **"Mommy and Me"** classes that it keeps **reasonably- priced** with the help of fundraising.

The **"drop-in"** times are popular as well, especially when it's crummy outside and you're aching to get out of the house. And if you're the mother of an **infant-toddler sibling combination**, the programs here are ideal; you'll find both the facility and the programs cater to the needs of **multi-aged children**.

If you want to test it out, call and find out about the **free parenting trial class** that's offered to prospective new members.

Parent Resource Center

232 Main Street, Suite 4, Port Washington
516-767-3808
www.parentresource.org

For new parents living in **Port Washington** and its environs, the Parent Resource Center is a terrific way to start your new life with baby on the right "foot-sie." Membership to this non profit cooperative entitles you to a smorgasbord of **baby classes**, adult **fitness classes** (with babysitting), and **social events,** with- and without - the kids.

Stay and Play

During the week, there are several hours of **"drop-in,"** when you and baby can turn up on the fly and hang out in a room full of toys with other parents and children. There's a **"drop-off"** schedule as well if you'd prefer some time to yourself, and at $5 an hour for babysitting, it's a bargain!

In fact, the center strives to **keep costs down** by obtaining grants and fundraising. As a **cooperative**, members are also expected to volunteer their time or services, be it baking cookies, or helping out at an event. If the price still seems prohibitive, the center also provides **financial assistance** to **low-income families** on a sliding scale.

Since the place is completely stroller-accessible, there's no reason not to **drop by with baby and check it out**. And you might appreciate knowing that after twenty plus years in operation, they have already served thousands of families in the Port Washington area.

Mothers of Twins Club

www.nomotc.org, go to 'Find a Club' and enter zip code
1-248-231-4480

I don't have twins but I can certainly appreciate the challenges unique to raising two or more same-aged children at a time. For parents blessed with double or *triple* the fun, the **National Organization of Mothers of Twins Club** (NOMOTC) offers plenty of opportunities to meet other big families in a social setting. The club is not just for parents of twins, any multiple is welcome. I have talked to several members who rave about the club's chapters in both Nassau and Suffolk.

Club activities include:

- Monthly Meetings
- New Member Gatherings
- Discussion Groups
- Holiday Parties
- Family Picnics
- Outdoor Playdates

Annual dues are $25-$35

Local NOMOTC Chapters:

Nassau
www.ncmotc.org
Meets in Hicksville

Suffolk
www.suffolktwins.org
Meets in Bohemia
631-574-4107

Making Playdates on the Web

     A great resource for moms with a computer, the internet is a gateway to groups of hundreds of fellow new parents living right here on the island. **Looking to form a playgroup in your town?** Post a message on one of the many websites designed specifically to bring new mothers together. You'll likely discover a world of like-minded people with young children looking to gather at **parks, shopping malls,** and other public places.

     You can also arrange to have the site's daily messages **emailed to you**. Depending on the message board however, that could translate into upwards of 50 emails a day, making you feel either very popular, or very overwhelmed. But the nice thing is that you can tailor your level of participation to *your* needs and schedule, and the service is completely **free**.

Websites to check out:

Yahoo! Groups usually has several Long Island sites to choose from. Some of the groups target specific audiences such as working moms or moms living in Babylon Ttownship. For a current list go to:

www.groups.yahoo.com
Then click on Family & Home > Moms > By Location > U.S. States > New York > New York City Metro > Long Island

Look for the groups with lots of members and lots of activity within the last 7 days. These tend to be the most active.

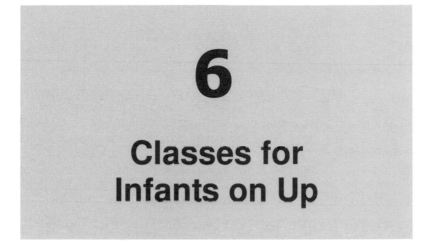

6

Classes for Infants on Up

What baby wouldn't want to go to a class called **"Mommy and Me?"** Whether you have an aspiring soccer player on your hands or painter, a gymnast or a nature lover, this chapter has information on a class to suit his or her tastes.

And even though the term to describe these interactive class for tiny tots has come to be known as "Mommy and Me," it's definitely a misnomer; **any adult caregiver** can, and should participate at least once! So come on down **dad, grandpa, big sis,** and **Aunt Betty too** – you'll find a whole host of other grown-ups besides mommies there, all having a great time **bonding with their babies and toddlers**.

Free Trial Classes

Some of these classes can be pricey and require signing up for ten or more sessions at a time, but before you get out your wallet find out if they offer a free trial class. Many places offer them and why not? Usually they are so good that parents do wind up signing up.

Choosing A Class

When I first heard there were "classes" for newborns, I was pretty skeptical. About all Ben could do then was drink his bottle and poop, what could he possibly gain from a class at that tender age? Naturally I was aware of the mountains of research out there on how important it is to expose baby to different experiences early on, but the idea of an infant taking "classes" seemed like overkill. Just for fun though I finally took him to The Little Gym when he was six months old.

To my surprise, not only did *he* enjoy it, but *I* did as well. Between **the music, the balls, and the bubbles**, the 45 minute session flew by. It was pretty social too and there was time to **chat with other parents** that potentially could lead to playdates.

At the more music-oriented classes, we also learned plenty of tunes to sing during long car rides. In fact, some of the programs include companion CDs or song books to encourage the learning to continue at home with baby. Especially during their first few months of life, I have found that songs and finger plays are invaluable ways to "communicate" and elicit smiles.

Will Your Child Throw a Tantrum?

A child's response to a class can be very unpredictable. For many babies, it's the first time they are in a structured environment. The presence of so many strangers, loud music, and colorful props could be delightful, or sensory overload. So it's important not to have any great expectations for baby's performance. I hope your baby will be the one that claps to the beat and enthusiastically follows the motions of the teacher.

134

But if they're anything like Ben was, they'll be up and dashing off to some corner with you in hot pursuit attempting to re-direct them back to the circle of participants.

As you discover what your child's likes and dislikes are, do keep one thing in mind – **what they love today may be what turns them off tomorrow.** So baby's lack of interest in an activity *now* should not deter parents from trying it again *later*. As you know, little ones can be very temperamental, and their enjoyment hinges on a number of factors including when they last ate or napped.

What If She Doesn't Share?

Since many of the classes have toys or other items to stimulate learning, baby will be presented with many opportunities to practice her "sharing" skills. My son Tycho was only seven months when a toy would become so dear to him that he would wail uncontrollably if you took it from his hands. (Of course, the second I gave it back, he would miraculously recover and shoot me one of his mischievous grins.)

Relatively speaking, younger babies tend to be easier to manage at these classes; try telling an impatient, whining *toddler* that they have to wait their turn to hold the "horsie" that another child is playing with. And when they finally get their hands on that precious horsie, try telling them to pass it to another child a few minutes later! But alas, sharing is something we all have to do eventually, and here youngsters can begin to learn the lessons of cooperating, working together and even negotiating that will clearly be a part of the rest of their lives.

Bring Socks!

Since many of the indoor activities require children and their caregivers to wear socks, it's wise to keep an extra pair in the car, especially in the summer when it's flip-flop season.

What Class is Right for You?

All the classes reviewed in this section are very good, and I'd be hard-pressed to try to rank them since so much also depends on the instructor and parent preferences. Since all the classes are generally comparable in price and quality, the most important factor in deciding which class to enroll my child in is driving distance.

That said, when weighing the pros and cons of different programs, you may also want to consider the following factors:

- How close is it to home? Do they allow **make-ups** for missed classes? Are the make-ups easy enough to do?

- Is **"open play"** offered to class participants at certain times during the week? It's a nice option if you like to get out of the house frequently with baby.

- What's included in the tuition? Some programs provide **books and CDs** to use at home.

- What is the policy on **siblings?** Are there discounts? Can infants come along with their toddler sibling?

- How's the **parking?** Close by and convenient?

- Are there classes on **weekends?** Many offer them for working parents.

- Do they offer **trial classes** for free (or at a fee) so you can get a flavor for what it's all about?

- If a free trial class is not an option, can you at least **observe** part of one?

Places to look

While there are literally hundreds of classes on the Island to choose from, this section focuses on the major franchises with established reputations and years of experience. In searching for something closer to home, it's worth shopping around for more local, "mom and pop" type operations; many of them offer terrific, not to mention more economical, programs. Here are the types of places to check.

- Fitness Centers
- Gymnastics Facilities
- Town Halls
- Preschools
- Mother Centers
- Museums
- State and County Parks
- Dance Studios
- Yoga Centers
- Libraries (free for residents!)

Classes Reviewed in This Chapter

Music, Movement, & Arts
- Gymboree
- Just Wee Two
- Kindermusik
- Music Together

Eco-Tot Adventures
- New York State Parks
- Caleb Smith State Park
- Connetquot River State Park
- Suffolk County Farm
- Alley Pond Environmental Center

Lil Jocks & 'Jockettes'
- Soccer Tots
- Lil Sluggers
- The Little Gym
- Sportime
- Saf-T-Swim
- The "Y" & JCC

Fitness for Mom
- Stroller Strides

Honorable Mentions
(reviewed in other chapters, see index for page # of review)
- Doodle Bugs Gym
- Little Sunshine Playcenter
- The Children's Safari
- Orly's Treehouse
- Once Upon a Treetop
- Children's Museum of East End
- Active Kidz
- Let's Bounce 'n' Party
- Pump It Up
- Center for Parents & Children
- Parent Resource Center

Gymboree

Multiple locations
1-877-449-6932
www.gymboree.com

Classes: Baby/toddler classes featuring music and movement, art classes beginning at 18 months, open gym times.

Age: Newborns on up.

Program: About 15 classes weekly.

Class Length: 45min - 1 hour depending on class.

Price: Differing packages; about $20 per class; monthly membership available for about $82 (one-time, $35 new member initiation fee).

Trying It: Most locations offer free trial classes.

The Scoop:

One of my favorite things about Gymboree is the space itself. The **bright, colorful room** is filled with soft, inviting mats and play equipment designed especially for little ones. The staff takes significant measures to keep it clean too, and will gently remind participants to **remove their shoes** before entering the play area.

It's amazing how many activities the instructors can cram into a 45 minute class, and how each activity targets a different aspect of the **child's development**. At one class for example, my 18 month son went "fishing" on a bridge where the object of the game was to hook aquatic creatures with a fishing pole. While Ben concentrated on reeling in the catch of the day, the instructor pointed out that the exercise developed **"fine motor skills"** and stimulated the imagination through **"pretend play."**

In a class for infants, the teachers will point out when the baby is being *visually* **stimulated** (by a rainbow-colored parachute fluttering overhead) or experiencing *tactile* **stimulation** (as a cotton ball is brushed lightly against their cheeks). The auditory aspect of this **"multi-sensory"** approach is demonstrated by the instructors themselves who sing with surprisingly good voices.

Gymborees in Nassau:

Great Neck
516-466-1308

Woodbury
516-367-3950

Westbury
516-542-6147

Oceanside
516-764-2659

Gymborees in Suffolk:

Oakdale
631-563-4154

St. James
631-979-2881

East Northport
631-368-2059

Just Wee Two

Manhasset, Plainview
516-433-0003, 800-404-2204
www.justweetwo.com

Activities: Toddler classes.

Age: 14 months on up.

Program: About 11 classes held once a week.

Class Length: 90 minutes.

Price: Around $37 per class.

Trying It: Some locations offer trial classes.

The Scoop:

At **90 minutes**, Just Wee Two's classes last longer than most, but its less-intense, more leisurely pace makes it a good choice for the toddler who prefers to take his time. But the staff still manages to get a whole lot of structured activity in, and a typical class will likely include:

- Open play in a room full of toys and music
- Supervised craft
- Story-time
- Song-filled circle time

Some classes feature a period of **"partial separation"** when the adults are ushered out of the room to allow the children to experience the world without a parent present. A few of the children whine a bit which is to be expected, but the majority of toddlers seem to have a blast with their newfound independence. So much for needing mommy all the time! Well it's just as well, and besides, it's nice to have a few uninterrupted minutes to flip through a magazine while your toddler prepares for the next stage of growing up – preschool!

Music Together

Locations throughout Long Island
800-728-2692
www.musictogether.com

Activities: Baby/toddler classes in music & movement.

Age: Newborn to 4 years.

Program: Around 11 classes held weekly.

Class Length: Typically 45 minutes long.

Price: Around $20 per class (plus one-time registration fee); includes kit with book & CD, sibling discounts.

Trying It: Free trials at select locations.

The Scoop:

For people who appreciate lively, festive music, Music Together offers a very catchy selection of songs to explore rhythms, tone, and beat with baby. Many of the Instructors play an instrument and you might hear anything from **Latin mambos, to R & B, to bluegrass.**

One of the nice aspects of Music Together is that the **classes are multi-aged.** Children from birth to four years share the space together, and I saw one energetic mom rocking her infant in her arms while bouncing her toddler on her knee! Go momma!

It's not just about *listening* **to the music**; throughout the class different instruments are brought out so everyone plays an active role in *making* **music.**

The tuition **includes a kit with a CD and songbook,** and parents are encouraged to learn the lyrics and sing out loud to their baby. Because new locations are opening all the time, call or check their website for a current listing of classes.

141

Kindermusik

Multiple locations
1-800-628-5687
www.kindermusik.com

Activities: Baby/toddler classes focusing on music and movement.

Age: Newborns on up.

Program: Varies by location; ranges from 8-15 classes held once a week.

Class Length: About 45 minutes.

Price: Around $15-$20 per class including kit (CD, book).

Trying It: Free trials at most locations; call for details.

Introducing babies and toddlers to the world of music for over two decades, Kindermusik has amassed a wealth of expertise in the area of **early childhood development**. During the class, licensed Kindermusik instructors guide the adult through a series of musical exercises to try with baby or toddler. There is **infant massage**, "dancing" with baby, and songs designed to facilitate language acquisition.

At a class I attended, two out of the five caregivers were **dads** and one of them seemed to feel a bit goofy skipping around the room making bird sounds. But gradually he grew less self-conscious as it became clear that the child was having fun.

If you have **two left feet**, this is actually a good place to learn a few dance steps to enjoy with baby. Also, the words to the songs are posted on the wall, and no one seems to mind if your voice cracks on the high notes like mine did. If you are totally mortified at such a public display of your musical talents, you can lip sync while you're there and take home the kit that's included with the tuition. It has a **CD, book,** and other props to practice with baby in the privacy of your living room. In fact the teacher even gives out *"homework assignments"* to help reinforce the skills taught in class.

Babies and their caregivers really do seem to enjoy these classes and I got so into it at one point that the instructor had to very sweetly inform me that my 4 month old son had just spit up part of his breakfast on the floor. But that's what babies do, and everything goes in the **laid back atmosphere** they create to emphasize the pleasure of music and movement. Some of the classes offered on Long Island are listed below, but since new instructors are cropping up all the time, it might serve you better to consult their website for a more current list.

Kindermusik in...

Nassau:

Hempstead
Young Musician Institute
www.ymimusic.com
516-564-4301

Manhasset
Music Institute of Long Island
516-627-7052
www.milimusic.com

Great Neck
Great Neck Music Conservatory
www.greatneckmusicconservatory.com
516-829-6084
With Holli-Ann Larocca,
516-466-3994

Suffolk:

Islip
Carol O'Neill
kindermusikbymusic4young.kind
ermusik.net
631 328 1548

St James
North Shore Academy Of Dance
631-899-4340

Lil Jocks & Jockettes

Though they're not headed for the Olympics anytime soon, even barely-toddling children can benefit from exercises aimed at developing **hand-eye coordination, gross motor skills, and balance**.

And while tossing a ball around the backyard with daddy is great, the experienced instructors at these classes have the **patience, enthusiasm and communication skills** to inspire your pee wee athlete.

They can also *teach the teacher*, that is, show parents a variety of **age-appropriate exercises** to practice with their children at home. In fact, it was at one of these classes that I learned how to spot my one-year old through a **forward roll**. It was so cute, I couldn't wait to show his dad when he came home from work that evening. Well not only did my husband get a kick out of watching Ben tumble, but he was also eager to **learn the technique** himself so he could join in the fun. I pointed out how to tuck Ben's head under so he could safely roll over, and Voila! Daddy had a new game to play with his son!

Soccer Tots

Multiple Locations
631-754-2257
www.soccertotslongisland.com

Activities: Soccer classes.

Age: 18 months – 6 years.

Program: Around 12 weekly classes, 50 minutes long.

Price: About $18 per class, sibling discounts.

Trying It: Free trial class, call for details.

The Scoop:

Toddlers get a 'kick' out of these classes which emphasize motor skill development and fitness. Parents will also get their kicks out of watching someone else try to get their child to pay attention and follow directions. The coaches are pretty effective though, and you may pick up a few tips.

Locations

Huntington Station
WEST
156 Railroad Street

Bethpage
Sportime Bethpage Multi Sport
1405 Hempstead Turnpike

Hauppauge
Matt Guiliano's Play Like A Pro
1745 Express Drive North

Setauket
World Gym Setauket
384 Mark Tree Street

Oceanside
Turf Island
3573 Maple Court

West Hempstead
Island Garden Basketball
45 Cherry Valley Avenue

Farmingville
KK Athletics
755 Horseblock Rd

Sayville
Interstate Sports Academy
264 N. Main Street

Bay Shore
Play Like A Pro Sports South
57 Park Avenue

Glen Cove
Cove Baseball
200 Carney Street

Lil Sluggers

Multiple Locations
631-367-9378
www.lilsluggersbaseball.com

Activities: Baseball classes.

Age: 2 – 5 years.

Program: ~12 weekly classes, 45 minutes long.

Price: About $20 per class, sibling discounts.

Trying It: Free trial class, call for details.

The Scoop:

For tots with developing motor skills, Lil Sluggers offers a fun introduction to the game of baseball. Watching them attempt to throw, catch and hit a wiffle ball is amusing, but the sight of them trying to round the bases is major league funny; half the time they shoot right past ending up somewhere in left field, and then coaches have their hands full trying to cajole them back to home base.

Locations

Oceanside
Turf Island
3573 Maple Ct

Farmingville
KK Athletics
755 Horseblock Rd

Sayville
Interstate Sports
246 N. Main St.

Glen Cove
Cove Baseball
200 Carney St

Bellmore
Sportsplex Bellmore
1329 Newbridge Rd

Huntington Station
WEST
156 Railroad St

Bay Shore
Play Like A Pro
57 Park Ave

East Setauket
World Gym
384 Mark Tree Rd.

Hauppauge
Matt Guiliano's Play Like A Pro
1745 Express Drive North

West Hempstead
Island Garden Basketball
45 Cherry Valley Ave

Saf-T-Swim

Throughout Long Island
1-866-SAFE-SWIM (1-866-723-3794)
www.safetyswim.com

Activities: Swimming lessons.

Age: Two months and up.

Program: Usually 4 weekly classes per session.

Class Length: 30 minutes.

Price: Depends on type of class.

Trying It: No trial classes offered but there are "viewing rooms" to observe a class in action.

The Scoop:

Even in the midst of a winter cold snap, you won't feel chilly going for a dip in these **warmer-than-bathwater** pools that host classes for babies as young as **two months**.

With only **half an hour** allotted for the class though, it feels like most of your time is spent either dressing or undressing yourself and baby. But most participants agree that the time in the pool is well spent and the instructors manage to squeeze in a surprising number of basic pre-swimming techniques that make the class both **enjoyable and educational**.

In general, the facilities are immaculate and decorated in playful aquatic themes that are very inviting for little ones. If you don't care to get your own feet wet though, you can always sign baby up for **individual lessons**. Then you can look on from the comfort of a separate viewing room as he or she tries to keep their head above water, or below, as the case may be.

Saf-T-Swim Locations:

Nassau

East Meadow
625 Merrick Ave
516-538-6900

Westbury
570 Main St
516-876-0848

Suffolk

Coram
1850 Rte 112
631-736-6604

Bohemia
3500 Vets Mem Hwy
631-580-2825

Commack
6136 Jericho Tpke
631-462-9696

Deer Park
1015 Grand Blvd
631-254-4025

Smithtown
7 Browns Road
Nesconset
631-406-7316

Riverhead
150-154 Kroemer Ave
631-727-5458

The Little Gym

Multiple Locations
888-228-2878
www.thelittlegym.com

Activities: Baby/toddler classes emphasizing motor skills.

Age: 4 months & up.

Program: Around 19 weekly classes.

Class Length: 45 min-1 hour.

Price: Around $20 per class.

Trying It: Free trial classes at most sites.

The Scoop:

As the name suggests, the classes offered at The Little Gym are very **fitness-oriented.** Soft cubes, ramps, balance beams, and other **gym equipment** create a colorful, not to mention irresistible, obstacle course for a child to explore. Activities are tailored to your little athlete's age and development, and set to cheerful music that keeps everyone grooving along.

One of the best aspects of taking a class there was learning how to guide baby through a few basic gymnastics moves that we could practice at home. The teachers understand a **baby's body limitations** and are happy to demonstrate exercises that even very small babies can enjoy **safely.**

The Little Gym Locations

Merrick	**Huntington**	**Port Washington**
2128 Merrick Mall	TBD	2C Soundview Market Pl
516-223-4008	631-360-7777	516-944-8346

Smithtown	**Sayville**
138 East Main St	5640 Sunrise Hwy
631-360-7777	631-563-0950

149

The "Y"
& JCC Community Centers

Multiple Locations

Better known for their adult fitness programs, these **community-oriented, recreational centers** offer a wide variety of programs tailored to the interests of diaper-wearing Long Islanders. While the JCC, which stands for **Jewish Community Center**, does maintain a religious identity supported by special programs to celebrate Judaism, people of all faiths are welcome, and it's worth checking out if you live in the area.

The enrollment policies differ by facility; some require baby to become a member while others allow you to sign up for sessions a la carte. Either way, the **adult need not be a member** for baby to participate.

To get a sense of their offerings, log on or order a program guide. Here's a small sample of what's cooking around the island:

- **Swimming lessons**
- **Infant massage**
- **Craft, story and song**
- **Pee Wee sports**
- **Mommy and baby yoga**
- **Stroller aerobics**

For those of us who aren't into multi-tasking with baby, many of the facilities provide **babysitting** freeing mom to focus on strengthening her abs without having to deal with whimpers or whines. Baby usually has to be at least six months of age and the hourly rates tend to be quite reasonable. But if you're just too exhausted to put on your spandex and bounce around, look for the **new mommy discussion groups** hosted at select locations.

Ys and JCCs in Nassau:

Barry & Florence Friedberg JCC
www.friedbergjcc.org
Oceanside Facility
15 Neil Court, Oceanside
516-766-4341
Long Beach Division
310 National Blvd, Long Beach
516-431-2929
Merrick Extension
22 Fox Blvd, Merrick
516-379-9386

JCC of the Greater Five Towns
207 Grove Ave, Cedarhurst
516-569-6733
www.fivetownsjcc.org

YMCA at Glen Cove
125 Dosoris Lane, Glen Cove
www.ymcali.org
516-671-8270

Mid Island Y-JCC
45 Manetto Hill Rd, Plainview
www.miyjcc.org
516-822-3535

Sid Jacobson JCC
300 Forest Dr, East Hills
www.sjjcc.org
516-484-1545

Ys and JCCs in Suffolk:

Brookhaven-Roe/East YMCA
155 Buckley Rd, Holtsville
www.ymcali.org
631-289-4440

Huntington YMCA
60 Main St, Huntington
www.ymcali.org
631-421-4242

YMCA East Hampton
2 Gingerbread Lane, East Hampton
www.ymcali.org
631-329-6884

Great South Bay YMCA
200 W. Main St, Bay Shore
www.ymcali.org
631-665-4255

Suffolk Y JCC
74 Hauppauge Rd, Commack
www.suffolkyjcc.org
631-462-9800

Sportime

Multiple locations
1-888-NYTENNIS, 1-888-698-3664
www.sportimetfm.com

Activities: Toddler and older classes geared toward learning sports.

Age: 2 years and up.

Program: Around 16 classes held weekly.

Class Length: 45 minutes to an hour depending on class.

Price: Around $20 per class.

Trying it: No trial classes offered.

The Scoop:

Sportime's athletic program for children, called **StartKids**, offers multi-sport classes to children **aged 2** and up that touch on a variety of sports including **baseball, soccer, and basketball.** Using props such as whistles and cones, the "coaches" guide toddlers through exercises that emphasize skills like **listening** and **following directions** as well as **hand-eye coordination.**

Sportime Locations:

Bethpage
4105 Hempstead Tpke
516-731-4432

Syosset
75 Haskett Dr
516-364-2727

Lynbrook
175 Merrick Rd
516-887-1330

Kings Park
275 Old Indian Head Rd
631-269-6300

The Hamptons
Rte 104, Quogue
631-653-6767

152

Eco-Tot Adventures

Your budding nature enthusiasts will adore the programs reviewed in this section, and the best part is that you don't have to commit to months of classes. You sign up for one session at a time, and working parents will find a selection of offerings that take place on the **weekend.**

New York State Park Programs

Throughout Nassau & Suffolk
Call 631-581-1072 to get on the mailing list
www.nysparks.state.ny.us

Activities: Nature Classes (Tiny Tots program).

Age: 3 years and up; younger siblings can come along and hang out.

Program: Single sessions, 1-1½ hours.

Several of the twenty or so New York State Parks on the island offer terrific **nature programs** that are a great bargain especially if you happen to have an Empire Passport sticker on your car window so the park entrance fee of $6 is waived. When deciding on which class to choose, either stick with the Tiny Tots program which are geared to ages 3 to 5, or call and inquire about how appropriate it is, given your children's ages. Some of the other family-centered programs may be too dull or tire little ones out with all the hiking involved.

Caleb Smith State Park & Museum

581 West Jericho Turnpike, (Rte 25), Smithtown
631-265-1054
www.nysparks.state.ny.us/parks
Program brochure mailing list: 631-581-1072

Activities: Nature Classes (outdoors if weather permits).

Age: 3 years & up; younger siblings can come along.

Program: Single sessions, about 1-1½ hours long.

Fees: Adults, free; children ages 3-17, $2; Under 3, free. In addition, $6 vehicle fee charged at gate; fee waived with Empire Passport sticker.

Finding It: LIE (495) to exit 53 north OR Southern State Pkwy to Exit 41A north; take Sunken Meadow Pkwy north to exit SM3. Go east to Smithtown via Jericho Tpke (Rte 25) for ~ 3 miles to park.

Parking: Park at lot by ticket booth. About a 3 minute walk uphill from lot to the main house.

Stroller: Stroller-accessible, plenty of stroller parking.

Bathrooms: Changing table in men's & ladies' restrooms.

Food: OK to bring sippy cups, bottles, toddler snacks. Park has a "carry in, carry out" policy for trash.

The Scoop:

Looking for a change of scenery? Check out the "Tiny Tots" class for ages 3-5. These nature programs are based in a **quaint house** overlooking a pond and surrounded by forest. The room layout for the classes is well suited to temperamental toddlers. Children having trouble sitting through the class can be shifted to an attached but separate space stocked with books and puzzles to keep them busy while they mellow out. Or they can take a peek into the **small museum** located in the same house.

154

Connetquot River State Park

Sunrise Highway, Oakdale, NY, Town of Islip
631-581-1005
www.nysparks.state.ny.us/parks
Program brochure mailing list: 631-581-1072

Activities: Nature classes, small visitor center.

Age: 3 years & up; younger siblings can come along.

Program: Generally single sessions, about 1-2 hours long.

Fees: Adults, free; children ages 3-17, $2; Under 3, free. In addition, $6 vehicle fee charged at gate; fee waived with Empire Passport sticker.

Finding It: Preserve located on north side of Sunrise Hwy, just west of Pond Rd. Take Sunrise Hwy to Oakdale and follow signs to preserve.

Parking: About 5 minute walk from lot to building.

Stroller: Strollers welcome, but there are a few steps to get into the building.

Food: OK to bring sippy cups, bottles, toddler snacks. Park has a "carry in, carry out" policy for trash.

The Scoop:

These **nature classes** are held in an elegant, historic mansion that once served as a Sportsmen Club whose well-heeled members fished the Connetquot River. House tours are offered, but are mainly of adult interest, and with the narrow passageways and steps, are no picnic with a toddler.

But the **"Tiny Tots" series**, tailored to ages 3-5, are wonderful. The park also offers "Fun for Kids" and "Family Adventures" programs which sound tempting, but are really geared to ages five and up. In addition to classes, there is a visitor center. It has several glass cases displaying local flora and fauna which are perfect for a game of **"I Spy" with toddler**. While they get busy trying to identify animals, you can look out the window and enjoy the **pretty river views**.

155

Suffolk County Farm
& Education Center

350 Yaphank Avenue, Yaphank
Suffolk, Town of Brookhaven
631-852-4600
www.cce.cornell.edu/suffolk
click on link for Suffolk County Farm

Activities: Interactive classes about life on the farm; live working farm area open to public for exploring; small playground-like area.

Age: Two years & up; infants allowed at "mixed age" classes; ideal for toddler/baby sibling combo.

Program: Sign up for one class or the whole series.

Class Length: About an hour.

Price: Around $10 per class, sibling discounts; farm grounds are free to visit and open year-round, daily, 9-3pm.

Finding It: LIE to exit 67; head south about ¼ mile and follow signs (it's also about ½ mile walk from Yaphank train station).

Food: No meals served; chips and soft drinks available at the gift shop; plenty of picnic tables to eat at if you bring a bag lunch from home.

The Scoop:

Taking a **class at a farm** has the advantages you would expect, that is, a whole host of activities centered around barnyard animals like **cows, sheep, and chickens.** If weather permits, the little ones will get to see them up close and personal, grazing behind the fences.

Unlike many of the other classes out there, you can **sign up for just one**, and the cost is very reasonable. They even have a class designed especially for the **infant-toddler sibling combo.**

The farm itself, which is free and open to the public year round, can be visited on its own, but keep in mind that the animals are a good 5-10 minute walk down a dirt path. At the gift shop you can pick up a map and let your child "find" the animals. The small playground with its stationary wooden train is also popular with the children.

Be sure to **reserve a space for the** classes; like all good things, they tend to fill up fast

```
================================
  Family Events

        Weekend  warriors  can
  take advantage of Family Fun
  Days that are held frequently in
  season.  A sampling of themes
  include  the  Spring  Scavenger
  Hunt, Baby Animal Day, and
  making crafts for dad on Father's
  Day.  Toddlers    can    usually
  participate in these events; call or
  log on to find out what's happening
  in the near future.
================================
```

Alley Pond Environmental Center

228-06 Northern Boulevard, Douglaston, Nassau/Queens border
718-229-4000
www.alleypond.com

Activities: Nature-oriented classes with live animals.

Age: 18 months & up, infants can accompany siblings for free as long as they stay in car seat.

Program: Varies, 1- 10 sessions, click on "Monthly Events" for more details.

Class Length: About 1-2 hours, depending on the class.

Price: Varies, about $15 - $20 per class.

The Scoop:

Though technically located in **Queens**, Alley Pond Environmental Center is just a stone's throw from the Nassau border near the convergence of the LIE and Grand Central Parkways. This nature center features a variety of **environmentally-oriented programs for children**, with some held on **weekends** to accommodate the schedules of **working parents.**

And what better way to enjoy a **Saturday together** than learning about the wonderful world of nature through fun, **hands-on activities**?

The Environmental Center is **open to the public year-round** and also has a small permanent display of live animals along with nature trails. But unless you live in the neighborhood, I would recommend visiting only if you're also signed up for a class.

Fitness for Mom

Moms looking to keep in shape have lots of options for exercising with baby. Many of the Y's and JCCs on the Island offer stroller aerobics, Mommy and Me yoga, and other fitness oriented classes. Another place to look is your local yoga studio; many offer classes where baby is welcome.

Another option to check out…

Stroller Strides

Various Locations in Nassau County
www.strollerstrides.com, click on 'Location'
347-677-2483

Activities: Fitness classes with baby in the stroller; free "Luna Moms" playgroups. See website for schedule.

Ages: Infants until as long as they can stand being in a stroller, about 3 years.

Class Length: 1 hour.

Price: $15/class; **1st class free**; $65 monthly membership for unlimited classes; other packages available.

The Scoop:

If you happen to be **at the mall** and see a woman wearing an Elmo hat and blowing bubbles at a dozen strollers, chances are you're witnessing a session of "Stroller Strides." The class provides a **total body workout** that combines power walking with intervals of body toning, all the while keeping baby entertained with songs and finger plays. Classes meet at parks in good weather and in the mall otherwise.

7

Additional Resources

Looking for more to do with baby? Check out the following websites and publications.

Newsday's Website

www.exploreli.com/entertainment/localguide/

Newsday has a great website featuring an interactive map of attractions by region with up to date event listings. You can also search by event type (choose kids) and narrow it down to the section of Long Island you live in.

Newsday's Parents & Children

www.liparent.com

Keep an eye out at your local library, daycare center, kids party place, or even CVS for "Newsday's Parents & Children," a **free** magazine with terrific articles about all things related to children. A look at their calendar of events reveals that there is something fun and interesting to do on Long Island just about every day of the month. Their resource guides, which are also online, provide comprehensive directories of everything from birthday party places, classes, and schools, to medical support.

Long Island Travel Guide

1-877-FUN-ONLI
www.licvb.com

Published by the Long Island Convention & Visitors Bureau, this **free, full-color guide** includes a comprehensive list of the Island's parks, beaches, museums and other attractions. Copies can be ordered by phone or through their website.

While you're on their website, have a look at their **Calendar of Events** which lists activities like festivals, children's programs, and shows.

Right in Town

If you haven't done so already, it's worth stopping by your **town hall**. I have found their departments of Parks and Recreation to be a terrific local resource for finding **inexpensive programs for young children** (subsidized by your tax dollars of course).

When you go, ask for any brochures or write-ups on nearby parks and beaches; I got a great **list of all my town beaches** that way with good driving directions and playground information.

8

Listings by Town

Nassau   **Suffolk**

North   Oyster   Huntington   Southold
         Bay
Hempstead   Smithtown   Riverhead
                                                                  East
     Hempstead   Babylon   Islip   Brookhaven   Southampton   Hampton

Nassau – North Hempstead

Active Kidz   98
210 Forest Dr. East Hills, Nassau
516-621-6600
www.activekidzlongisland.com
Activities: Open play, classes for ages 1-8

Alley Pond Environmental Center   158
228-06 Northern Blvd, Douglaston
718-229-4000
www.alleypond.com
Activities: baby/toddler classes, outdoor trails, live animals

Barnes & Noble   122
1542 Northern Blvd, Manhasset, 516-365-6723
91 Old Country Rd, Carle Place, 516-741-9850
1424 Union Tpke, New Hyde Park, 516-437-0324
www.barnesandnoble.com
Activities: children's section, story time at select locations

Borders Books   122
1260 Old Country Rd, Westbury, 516-683-8700
www.borders.com
Activities: children's section, story time at select locations

Doodle Bugs Gym   99
145 Voice Rd, Carle Place
516-747-9120
Activities: baby/toddler classes, open play

Garvies Point Museum & Preserve   78
50 Barry Dr, Glen Cove
516-571-8010/11
www.co.nassau.ny.us/parkmuse.html
Activities: exhibits at toddler eye level and of adult interest

Great Neck Plaza   62
Middle Neck Rd and Bond St, Great Neck
Activities: Nice town for strolling and window shopping

Gymboree   138
Great Neck, 516-466-1308
Westbury, 516-542-6147
www.gymboree.com
Activities: baby/toddler classes, open play at select locations

Just Wee Two   140
1845 Northern Blvd, Manhasset
516-433-0003
www.justweetwo.com
Activities: Toddler classes

JCC (Sid Jacobson Jewish Community Center)   151
300 Forest Dr, East Hills
516-484-1545
www.sjjcc.org
Activities: baby/toddler classes

Nassau – Hempstead

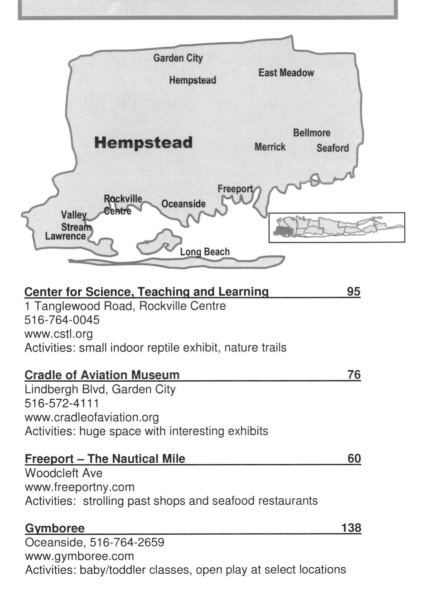

Center for Science, Teaching and Learning   95
1 Tanglewood Road, Rockville Centre
516-764-0045
www.cstl.org
Activities: small indoor reptile exhibit, nature trails

Cradle of Aviation Museum   76
Lindbergh Blvd, Garden City
516-572-4111
www.cradleofaviation.org
Activities: huge space with interesting exhibits

Freeport – The Nautical Mile   60
Woodcleft Ave
www.freeportny.com
Activities: strolling past shops and seafood restaurants

Gymboree   138
Oceanside, 516-764-2659
www.gymboree.com
Activities: baby/toddler classes, open play at select locations

Nassau – Oyster Bay

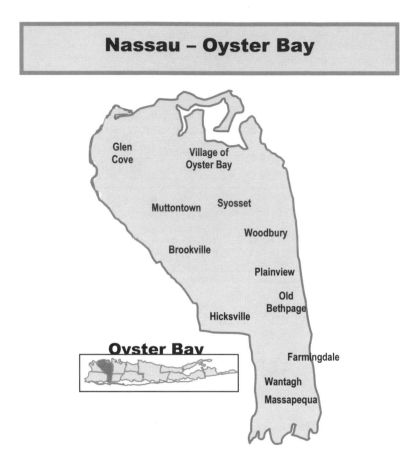

Barnes & Noble 122
5224 Sunrise Hwy, Massapequa
516-541-1456
www.barnesandnoble.com
Activities: children's section, story time at select locations

Borders Books 122
425 Jericho Tpke, Syosset, 516-496-3934
231 Airport Blvd, Farmingdale, 631-752-0194
460 Sunrise Mall, Massapequa, 516-795-3683
www.borders.com
Activities: children's section, story time at select locations

Suffolk – Town of Huntington

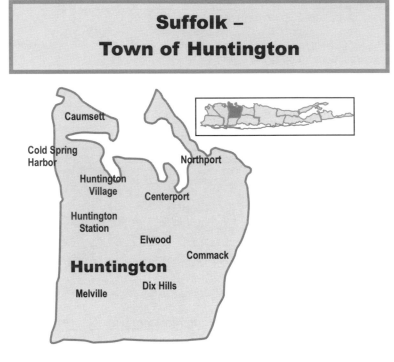

Barnes & Noble 122
380 Walt Whitman Rd, Huntington Station, 631-421-9886
4000 E. Jerciho Tpke, East Northport, 631-462-0208
www.barnesandnoble.com
Activities: children's section, story time

Book Revue 122
313 New York Ave (Rte 110), Huntington
631-271-1442
www.bookrevue.com
Activities: browsing books with baby, story time

Caumsett State Historic Park 30
25 Lloyd Harbor Rd, Huntington
631-423-1770
Activities: paved paths for strolling or biking with baby

Suffolk –
Town of Babylon

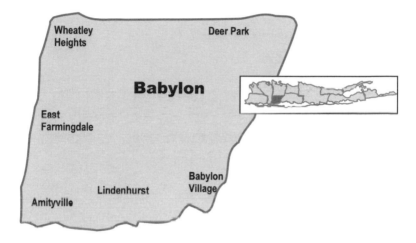

Wheatley Heights

Deer Park

Babylon

East Farmingdale

Lindenhurst

Babylon Village

Amityville

Kangaroo Kids   **108**
1015 Grand Blvd. Deer Park
631-871-8762
www.kangarookidsparty.com
Activities: open play, indoor inflatable party space

La Leche League   **127**
847-519-7730
www.lalecheleague.org
Activities: breastfeeding support group

Let's Bounce 'N' Party   **106**
602 N. Wellwood Ave, Lindenhurst
631-226-8623
www.letsbouncenparty.com
Activities: open play, indoor inflatable party space, classes

Suffolk –
Town of Smithtown

Barnes & Nobles   122
5001 Jericho Turnpike, Commack
631-462-0896
www.barnesandnoble.com
Activities: children's section, story time at select locations

Borders Books   122
68 Veterans Memorial Highway, Commack
631-462-0569
www.borders.com
Activities: children's section, story time at select locations

Suffolk –
Town of Islip

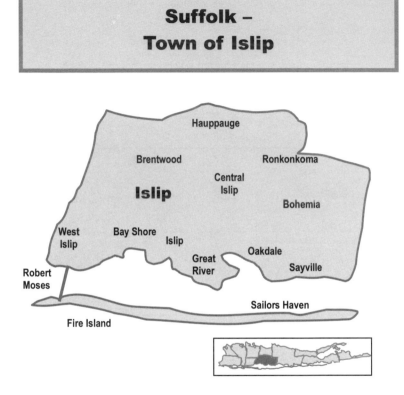

Barnes & Noble   122
42 Sunrise Hwy, Bay Shore
631-206-0198
www.barnesandnoble.com
Activities: children's section, story time at select locations

Bayard Cutting Arboretum   28
Montauk Hwy, Oakdale
631-581-1002
www.bcarboretum.com
Activities: Pretty grounds

Saf-T-Swim   147
55 West Main St, Bay Shore, 631-968-5253
3500 Vets. Memorial Hwy, Bohemia, 631-580-2825
www.safetyswim.com
Activities: swimming lessons

Sailors Haven, Fire Island   49
Ferry Leaves from Sayville
Visitor Center: 631-597-6183
www.nps.gov/fiis
Activities: ferry ride to island; beach, nature trail

Soccer Tots   145
Matt Guiliano's Play Like A Pro, 1745 Express Dr. N., Hauppauge
World Gym Setauket, 384 Mark Tree Street, Setauket
Interstate Sports Academy, 264 N. Main Street, Sayville
Play Like A Pro Sports South, 57 Park Avenue, Bay Shore
631-754-2257
www.soccertotslongisland.com

The Little Gym   149
5640 Sunrise Hwy, Sayville
631-563-0950
www.thelittlegym.com
Activities: baby/toddler classes

Suffolk –
Town of Brookhaven

Setauket Port Jefferson
Stony
Brook
Rocky
Point
Lake
Grove Coram
Lake
Ronkonkoma Medford
Yaphank Manorville
Holtsville
Brookhaven
Shirley
Patchogue

Animal Farm Petting Zoo   14
Wading River Rd, Manorville
631-543-7804
www.afpz.org
Activities: petting zoo, toddler play areas, shows

Barnes & Noble   122
600 Smith Haven Mall, Lake Grove
631-724-0341
www.barnesandnoble.com
Activities: children's section, story time at select locations

Suffolk –
Riverhead, Southold
& the Hamptons

Atlantis Marine World   16
431 East Main St, Riverhead
631-208-9200
www.atlantismarineworld.com
Activities: marine life viewing and shows

BookHampton   122
20 Main St, East Hampton, 631-324-4939
91 Main St, Southampton, 631-283-0270
20 Main St, Sag Harbor, 631-725-8425
Amagansett Square, 154 Main St. Amagansett, 631-267-5405
www.bookhampton.com
Activities: baby-friendly children section

Index of Places

Index of Places

Index of Places

ORDER FORM

District/Company: _____ Daytime Phone: _____

Name: _____

Address:_____

City:_____ State:_____ Zip:_____

Email: _____

Quantity	Description	Unit Price	Parent/ Non-Profit Groups	SCOPE Member District Price*		Total Price
	Baby Friendly Long Island	$11.95	$10.95	$8.95		
					Subtotal	
					S & H (taxable)	
	*Call 631.881.9650 to check if your school is a SCOPE member district				NYS Sales Tax 8.625%	
					Total	

Please call for quantity discount pricing (30 or more publications)

METHOD OF PAYMENT (check appropriate box below):
☐ Check, **payable to SCOPE**, enclosed ☐ Visa/MC/AMEX/Discover ☐ Purchase Order #_____

Card Number: _____ - _____ - _____ - _____

Card Holder Name: _____

Card Expiration Date: _____ Amount Charged: $_____

Card Holder Address **(if different from above)** _____

_____

_____

Card Holder Signature: _____

Shipping & Handling	
1 copy	$ 4.95
2-5 copies	5.50
6-10 copies	6.50
11-15 copies	7.50
16-20 copies	8.50
21-25 copies	9.50
26-30 copies	10.50
31 or more	CALL

MAIL Order To:
SCOPE Publications, Order Department
100 Lawrence Avenue
Smithtown, NY 11787

FAX Order To:
631.881.9672

For information on other SCOPE Publications, call Karen Wolff at 631.881.9650

Revised 4/28/09